Cooking Wild in Missouri

savoring the Show-Me State's game, fish, nuts, fruits and mushrooms

Bernadette Dryden

Serving nature and you

Missouri Department of Conservation

Front cover: *Missouri "Crab" Cakes* (see page 104)

All photographs by the author unless noted.
Edited by Bonnie Chasteen and Matt Seek
Designed by Marci Porter

Serving nature and you

ISBN 978-1-887247-77-1

Published by the Missouri Department of Conservation
P.O. Box 180, Jefferson City, Missouri 65102-1080

Dedication

To my mother, Opal Dryden, who gave me
my most important life gift—
teaching me to cook with love for those I love

Cooking Wild in Missouri

contents

introduction

what this book is and isn't

The seed for this cookbook was sown in 2003 when Karen Hudson, the Conservation Department's marketing specialist, asked if I would consider writing a cookbook in response to frequent public requests for a contemporary collection of fish and game recipes. Having edited many books for the Conservation Department throughout the years, I declined (knowing what an exhaustive process was involved in the making of any book). Besides, the Department already had a cookbook—and a very popular and utilitarian one, at that. Written in 1959 by the late Werner O. Nagel, *Cy Littlebee's Guide to Cooking Fish & Game* has sold thousands of copies in the last half century and is in its 17th printing. Why would we want to compete with such a successful product and one so charmingly written in the vernacular of The Ozarks? Perhaps most troubling to me was the fact that I was a forager, not a hunter or angler. I dismissed Karen's request, and the idea stayed just that for many years.

Karen, however, was relentless in her pursuit of a new cookbook, and I eventually caved in. I did, after all, have several decades of well-respected cooking experience to offer, which we decided was the most important qualification for authoring a cookbook. I also set some goals, from which I hope not to have wavered during the long process of writing, recipe-testing and photographing. My aim is to give Missourians a collection of recipes for cooking native foods in a variety of ways—primarily with whole, fresh and seasonal ingredients. There are a handful of recipes that call for deep frying, but most employ braising, poaching, sautéing, grilling and baking as cooking methods. Several require no heat at all. I have a deep respect for all the cuisines of the world (and a great love for a few, in particular), so I have reinterpreted and included dishes that reflect the diversity of many cultures. Missouri's game, fish, nuts, fruits and mushrooms adapt beautifully to recipes from Argentina to Zambia.

I also intend for this book to reflect proudly upon the state's native culinary traditions by giving voice to people involved in the producing and procuring of local foods. Consequently, I interviewed nut growers, mushroom and fruit foragers, hunters and anglers. I wanted to know what motivated them to spend hours in a cold trout stream, hunt deer with a bow, forage for obscure mushrooms, pick persimmons and pawpaws, and seek out bottomland hickory nuts.

This recipe collection is by no means a complete compendium of all the ways to cook Missouri's native plants and animals. It doesn't include wild greens and many other plants, for instance. *Wild Edibles of Missouri*, by Jan Phillips, has many recipes covered in that genre, and the book is available online via the Conservation Department's website. I also didn't include several game animals, such as woodcocks and woodchucks, that are hunted less frequently than others. There are many dishes I wanted to try, and would have had I not run out of time.

Please know that none of these recipes are strict formulas. Consider them as starting points for your own inspirations and interpretations. The dishes will become yours, as much as they have become mine, and as much as they were the cooks' who came before me.

a cooking philosophy and a way of life

I've always been inspired by words attributed to James Beard, the late, great dean of American cooking: "You can be fat, old and ugly, but if you know how to cook, you'll always have friends." I've found out—at least on one or two of those counts—that he was right. Throughout my 40-year cooking career, I've found that my best friendships, business relationships and other kinds of human interactions have started and been solidified over delicious food—cooked with love by people who care about its origin and outcome.

I consider cooking the most important life lesson that I learned from my mother. She proved that simple, grassroots dishes can be wonderful, and that any food cooked with love and care and the freshest, best-quality ingredients possible can be superb—be it cornbread or crêpes. That must be why most of my happiest childhood memories are tied to food—the bean soups and chilis of Monday wash days, the angel-food birthday cakes cooling off upside-down on tall 7-Up bottles on the back porch, the blackberry cobblers bubbling in the oven, and my uncle's freshly fried catfish hot from the skillet.

Food was a great participatory activity in our family. On the rare occasions we weren't fighting, my brother and I would spend hours together shucking ears of sweet corn in the summer or cracking hickory nuts on a little chunk of railroad track in the fall. My mom and I spent many a spring morning collecting wild greens in the field behind our house, and hot summer evenings stringing green beans or peeling peaches on the front-porch swing. At Christmastime, as she finished up one of her fabulous applesauce cakes or date puddings, I would stand over the "drinking custard" pot on the stove—helping myself to hot, sweet spoonfuls. When done, we'd carry the pot outside to the well top, where it would cool in the frigid air. A few hours later, my dad and I would take turns spooning up the skiff of frozen-custard deliciousness on top.

My food-loving family loved to get together on every holiday. We used these occasions as excuses to cook and eat all kinds of wonderful things. Equally important, the kitchen and dining-room tables became places where outlandish stories were told and family history was learned.

In addition to the cooking skills I inherited from my mother, I absorbed a lot from the women and men in the small Missouri Scots-Irish/German community where I grew up. The town churches' homemade ice-cream socials and dinners—replete with German potato salads, homemade sausages, Southern-style pimento-cheese and chicken-salad sandwiches, and ice cream with fresh strawberries—helped lay the foundation on which I built a passion for the cooking of various cultures.

Those experiences taught me that food was a fundamental part of my community's cultural identity, and that the dishes I tasted at those social functions and in the homes of neighbors were a result of knowledge passed down through generations of family cooks. Food, in fact, is a fundamental part of every community's cultural identity. What we eat, as individuals and as a community, helps define who we are and how we are connected (or not) to the land upon which we live.

We have to eat to live, so why not enjoy food to its fullest, including learning where it comes from and how to prepare it? Every act of cooking reaffirms the astonishing bounty of the Earth—the products of its forests, prairies, fields, rolling hills, mountains, rivers, lakes and oceans. Preparing fresh food not only inspires reverence for nature, but for the farmers who grow it. That reverence, in turn, cultivates consciousness and care in our actions.

Many of us work in jobs that don't produce tangible or visible goods, and disconnect us from nature in so many ways. One of the many reasons cooking is so wonderful is that there is always a product to show for your work and you get to eat it. Furthermore, if you pursue fresh, local and seasonal foods, you'll inevitably find yourself out in nature.

It's never too late to learn or too early to begin. In fact, why not give your children a lifelong gift? Teach them to hunt, fish and forage—and, of course, to cook. I guarantee that those lessons learned in nature and in the kitchen will serve them throughout their lifetimes as much as those learned on sports fields or in dance classes.

It gives me great satisfaction to pass forward some of my food and cooking knowledge to a younger generation. My volunteer experience with elementary-school children has shown me just how far a little effort can go. Every month we introduce a class of second or third graders to fresh, seasonal and local food, and the farmers who produce it. We cook with the students and watch their delight as they discover new taste sensations and experience the joys of turning raw products into delicious dishes. They walk away happy, with a new respect for where food comes from and for the people who grow it.

I hope you enjoy this collection of my cooking experiences. If you do, please pass on what you learn to the people you love, especially children; they are the future of food.

Bernadette Dryden

acknowledgments

I racked up a lot of debts from friends and colleagues at the Missouri Department of Conservation during the "sausage making" of this book, and owe the following people deep gratitude.

Karen Hudson, marketing specialist, conceived the idea for this project and was head cheerleader throughout the effort. Thanks for your friendship, relentless support and belief in my cooking and writing abilities. Lorna Domke, former Outreach and Education division chief, was a gracious supporter of the project, as were former supervisors Kirk Keller and Regina Knauer.

I am especially grateful to Kevin Lohraff, education programs supervisor, who not only shared recipes and many coolers of fish and game for my cooking experiments, but also was just as generous with his immense knowledge of animals and the natural world. Other suppliers of recipes and game to whom I owe thanks include colleagues Libby Block, Tim James, Jim Low, Mark Raithel and Dave Urich; friends Steve Brownlee and Barbara Leslie; and neighbors Gunilla and Dave Murphy.

Editors Bonnie Chasteen and Matt Seek deserve deep bows for improving the manuscript and giving me support in many other ways. Libby Block, my trusted assistant for 19 years, has been a pillar of support and has helped in more ways than I can count. Designer Marci Porter, whose talents and great patience are equally praiseworthy, brought stylish form to the text and photographs.

Other people who generously shared their time and knowledge with me include Lynn Barnickol, Steve Booker, Walker Claridge, Craig Cyr, Terry Durham, Theresa Ferrugia, Les Fortenberry, Mike Gold, Brook Harlan, Joe Holterman, Don Kurz, Kevin Lanahan, Mary Lyon, Joan McKee, John Schneller, Byron Smith, Maxine Stone, Julie Walker, Cliff White and David Yates.

To my family and close friends I owe much appreciation for enduring long periods of minimal contact during the book making. They supported me in the process by graciously conceding to my need for long bouts of solitary computer confinement. Thanks goes, especially, to all who were dutiful guinea pigs during the many meals that resulted from recipe testing. Barbara Bassett, Sally Beattie, Sue Bliss, Dory Colbert, Jan Colbert, Sarah Cyr, Harrell Dryden, Martha Folk, Michel Gregory, Miriam Hasenclever, Kathy Love and Sallee Purcell—thanks for putting up with me. John Stewart, you are in a class by yourself. Thanks for your good appetite, support and continuous patience while you shared the many culinary and emotional trials of this process.

I'd also like to thank the writers of cookbooks and food magazines past and present, and the farmers, food artisans, cooks and mentors in kitchens throughout the world for helping turn the Earth's bounty into delicious and inspired edible creations.

Last, but not least, I thank the Slow Food organization and all the other organizations, writers, filmmakers, food enthusiasts, cooks and activists who have given a voice to the sustainable food movement—of which Missouri's hunters and anglers are an important part. Thanks to all of you for helping preserve our culinary heritage.

Each month during the school year, Slow Food Katy Trail—the mid-Missouri chapter of Slow Food USA—introduces local and seasonal food to children at a Columbia elementary school. During these Harvest-of-the-Month sessions, local farmers bring in their products and share with the children what it's like to live on a farm and how they grow or produce their food. The children study the various foods in different areas of the curricula such as history, art and science. Local chefs and Slow Food volunteers accompany the farmers to help the children turn the farmers' products into delicious and nutritious treats.

A volunteer helps a second grader (left) flip pancakes made with freshly ground wheat grown in Callaway County. The cakes were topped with Boone County maple syrup and southern Missouri pecans. She—along with 60 other classmates—ground the wheat, made the pancakes and savored the results.

Slow Food is an eco-gastronomic, non-profit organization that seeks to reconnect people with the farmers, traditions, plants, animals, soils and waters that produce their food.

why seasonal and local foods make sense

As anglers, hunters and foragers, we take pride in eating what we have harvested and care considerably about the quality of the fish, meat or wild edibles we bring home. Being conservationists, we also care about the water quality of the lakes and rivers and the health of the forests where we pursue our sports. We spend no small amount of time keeping current on our passions, a fair amount of money on gear, and sometimes considerable effort in getting to and from our favorite fishing, hunting or foraging spots.

It seems reasonable, then, that we should care just as much about the integrity of the ingredients that complement our wild game meals. If you grow your own vegetables and fruits, purchase locally and organically whenever you can, or make weekly trips to your community's farmers market, then you know what I'm talking about. However, if the importance of any of these activities seems a little trivial, then please consider reading just a bit more.

To be true conservationists and environmentalists, it seems to me, we have to care about how *all* our food is grown and produced. Just as hunting, fishing and foraging sharpen our passion for nature and connect us to the creatures and plants that it supplies, so should the procurement of the rest of our food connect us to its producers. As we have become increasingly distant from the sources of what we eat, we seldom ask who grows our food, how the soil and crops are treated (and by consequence, the nearby waters), how the animals and the farm workers are affected by production methods, whether or not money spent for food goes to local farmers and gets circulated back into the community, or how our health is affected. All these things should matter to us.

Of the many reasons to eat locally grown and sustainably raised food, environmental impact is high on the list. When you purchase food from local producers, you are helping to preserve open space and wildlife habitat. When farmers get paid more for their products by selling them locally, they're less likely to sell farmland—and the wildlife habitat it contains—for development. Well-managed farms also conserve fertile soil and clean water in our communities.

When you buy locally raised food, you'll also be getting the freshest and tastiest food possible; few will disagree that produce picked at the height of freshness has more flavor. Additionally, you'll benefit from more interesting varieties. Local farmers are not limited to the few varieties that are bred for long-distance shipping, high yields and extended shelf life.

Buying locally also builds community; those who buy locally develop insight into harvest seasons and the land on which the food grows. Local food systems also provide an opportunity for education because they allow access to a place where people can go to learn about nature and agriculture.

Eating fresh, seasonal foods and buying them, when possible, from local growers we know and trust ensure that we become co-producers instead of consumers. When we educate ourselves about how our food is produced and actively support those who produce it, we become a part of and a partner in the production process. Something that helps me remember to practice what I preach is being conscious of the fact that every time I buy food, I'm casting a vote for how my food is grown. Ultimately, we all forge our connections between plate and planet by voting with our forks.

> "Get to know local farmers at farmers markets and by visiting their farms. Food tastes better when you've shaken the hand of the person who has grown it."
>
> —BCD

freshly ground spices make a difference

You may use pre-ground spices in these recipes. However, I believe that ground spices tend to lose their wallop when stored over time. Consequently, I keep whole spices in my pantry and grind them as needed. I use either a small, marble mortar and pestle or an electric coffee-bean grinder reserved specifically for spice grinding. It takes only a few extra minutes, but the resulting flavors are brighter and worth the small amount of effort. I usually grind spices while I'm waiting for onions to simmer or something else to finish cooking.

That said, I do keep on hand small quantities of coarsely ground black pepper, various types of New Mexican chile powders and a few kinds of ground cinnamon.

My "can't live without" spices are listed in *Stocking Your Kitchen* on page 14.

the importance of an herb garden

Intermingled among my flower and vegetable gardens are a couple of spaces—no more than 15 or 20 square feet total—that I've dedicated to herbs, which I consider a must for the creative cook. Fresh herbs make all the difference in the world. They lift an ordinary dish into the realm of the sublime.

Chives, oregano, marjoram, thyme, flat-leaved parsley, dill, basil, tarragon, rosemary and mint live happily together and add immeasurably to my cooking efforts. I encourage all cooks to grow as many of these herbs as possible, and as physically close to their kitchens as feasible. A few steps outside—and a few snips later—and you'll have what you need to season most dishes.

Nearly all of them are perennials, too, and require little effort. Dill is an annual, but reseeds like crazy. Parsley, a biennial, needs to be replanted every couple of years; however, any time spent on it is a good investment when you consider its versatility and the many tasty returns it provides. Rosemary needs indoor protection from Missouri winters, and basil must be started from seed each year. Give mint its own space or container because it tends to spread rapidly. Add Thai basil or lemongrass in the spring if you have room, in anticipation of flavoring Asian dishes later in the summer.

Some years are mild enough that I harvest herbs right through Thanksgiving. Before they get nipped by the first hard frost, however, I clip clusters of many of them for drying indoors. I tie a string around the stems and hang them upside down until the leaves are dry enough to flake into individual storage containers. Fresher and more flavorful than dried herbs you can buy, they're also less expensive and will hold you over until the mother plants awaken the next spring.

Only the sight of serviceberry blooming in the woods can fill me with more of a promise of spring than does the sight of chives poking through my garden soil on a blustery March day. I know then that the redbuds and dogwoods aren't far behind, and neither are the other herbs in the garden that contribute so much to the pleasures of eating.

stocking your kitchen

Second in importance to a freezer filled with fish and game is a well-stocked kitchen. Setting up and maintaining pantry shelves lined with essentials is the first step to creative and efficient cooking. Having to run to the market for items (other than fresh produce) every time you get the urge to cook is a big disincentive. Keeping certain basics on hand will help you avoid many last-minute trips for things that could be living happily on your shelves instead of on the store's. It also will make it easier to prepare a meal on the fly when unexpected company shows up. Most items in the following list are those that are needed for recipes in this book, but I've included some other things that are always in my kitchen. I choose local and organic products whenever available.

in the fridge

Apples (Missouri-grown)
Butter (unsalted, with extra in freezer)
Cheese (including whole wedges of Parmigiano-Reggiano and Pecorino Romano; Fresh Missouri goat)
Cilantro
Dairy (local cream and milk)
Eggs (local)
Ginger root
Horseradish
Lemons and limes
Nuts (including pine nuts, almonds, filberts, peanuts and Missouri pecans, walnuts and hickory nuts)
Parsley
Vegetables (including fresh local carrots, lettuce, spinach, kale, broccoli and other cole plants)

within easy reach of your cutting board

Garlic cloves
Onions (red and yellow)
Potatoes (white and sweet)
Shallots
Winter squash

in the pantry

Anchovies
Artichoke hearts
Asian noodles of various widths
Baking soda and powder
Canned beans (including garbanzo, cannellini, black and kidney)
Capers
Chicken stock
Chocolate (Missouri-made dark chocolate bars; the Show-Me State has two fine chocolate makers)
Coconut milk
Cornmeal (coarsely ground yellow and white)
Cornstarch
Dried beans, peas and lentils
Dried fruits (including dates, figs, white raisins, cranberries and tart cherries)
Dried mushrooms (assorted)
Dried pasta (including several widths of long noodles and a wide variety of shapes)
Dry sherry
Flours (unbleached white and whole-wheat)
Hoisin sauce
Honey (Missouri-made)
Maple syrup (Missouri-made)
Mirin (sweet rice wine)
Mustards (assorted, including Dijon)
Olives (assorted black and green, including Calamata, Nicoise, picholines, Cerignola)
Oils (assorted, including extra virgin olive oils, vegetable, walnut and peanut)
Oyster sauce
Peanut butter (100 percent pure peanut; plain and crunchy)
Peppers (jars of fire-roasted red and yellow)
Rice (white and brown short-grained and long-grained)
Rice papers for spring-roll making
Sesame oil (toasted)
Sorghum (Missouri-made)
Soy sauce
Sugars (assorted unrefined)
Sundried tomatoes
Sushi ginger
Tahini
Tamari

Thai fish sauce
Tomatoes (including canned whole, diced and
    diced fire-roasted)
Tomato paste
Vinegars (assorted, including balsamic,
    sherry, brown rice, red wine and cider)
Wasabi
Wines (dry reds and whites)
Worcestershire sauce
Yeast

dried spices and herbs

(All spices whole unless noted)

Allspice
Anise seeds
Basil (fresh frozen from your garden is best)
Bay leaves
Caraway seeds
Cardamom
Cayenne pepper (ground)
Chile oil
Cinnamon (whole sticks, plus small
    quantities of good-quality ground)
Cloves
Coriander
Cream of tartar
Crystallized ginger
Cumin seeds
Curry powder (best to blend your own)
Dill seed
Dill weed
Extracts (pure vanilla and almond)
Fennel seeds
Fenugreek
Ginger powder (fresh root is best, however)
Hot sauce (variety, including chipotle)
Lavender buds
Marjoram leaves
Mustard powder (Colman's brand)
Mustard seeds (black and yellow)
Nutmeg
Oregano leaves
Paprika (regular and Spanish smoked)
Rosemary leaves
Peppercorns (black, white, pink and green)
Pepper (coarsely ground black)
Pepper (red and green ground New Mexican;
    assorted Mexican whole; flakes)
Poppy seeds
Sage leaves
Sea salt (various kinds; coarse and fine)
Saffron threads
Sesame seeds (white and black)
Star anise
Tarragon leaves
Thyme leaves
Turmeric powder
Vanilla beans

long doesn't mean difficult

I suggest reading through a recipe completely before dismissing it as complicated. Even though a long list of ingredients may look intimidating, often the number of items is converse to the complexity of the dish. Remember that bread, which has only four primary ingredients (flour, yeast, salt and water) can be one of the most difficult things to make well. On the other hand, recipes with many spices (and other easily thrown-in items) can be among the quickest to put together.

Bernadette's Catch-All Muffins, page 120

Venison, rabbit and squirrel

venison, rabbit and squirrel
woods-to-table taste sensations

During the most recent firearms deer season, hunters harvested more than 230,000 whitetails in Missouri—about a quarter of the state's estimated deer population. Although deer is the most sought-after game animal in the state (turkeys are second), Missourians also enjoy bringing to the table a fair number of squirrels, rabbits and other small game.

I've often wondered how many more people would hunt and fish if they educated themselves about the origins of what they eat. Often stunned by negative responses about hunting from otherwise reasonable and educated carnivorous friends and acquaintances, I sometimes get feisty and challenge their notions regarding the sport.

I've known hunters and anglers all my life and worked with hundreds of them during my 23 years with the Conservation Department. I've always admired the strength, skill, stealth and patience it takes to draw back a bow, deftly cast a line or sit motionless in a cold deer stand for hours.

However, when I became involved in the Slow Food movement during the last decade, my appreciation for these sportsmen and women deepened even more. As I educated myself about our industrialized food system, learning how production animals are raised and our crops are grown—to say nothing of the dismal state of the nation's public school-lunch program—my respect for those who harvest their own food, especially meat, has done nothing but rise. Hunter-gatherers of the world are the true locavores—those who pursue the local animals and plants of the season, harvesting them at their prime and in their natural environments.

Of all the arguments I've read in support of harvesting one's own meat, journalist and food activist Michael Pollan makes one of the most eloquent in his book, *The Omnivore's Dilemma.* Among a wealth of salient points about the origins of our food, Pollan not only underscores hunting as the most humane and environmentally friendly way to obtain protein for the table, he also sheds light upon how most agricultural animals are prepared for consumption in this country. He suggests that were the walls of our meat industry transparent (literally or figuratively), we might find the idea of buying meat in foam and plastic containers much less appealing.

Kevin Lohraff, a Conservation Department colleague from whom I've learned much about the natural world, concurs. "Hunting is one of the most natural things I know," he says. "For me it is the ultimate connection between the land you live on and yourself. It also gives you an intimate connection with what you put in your body."

The meat and fish that Kevin and his family eat are almost exclusively from animals that he harvests from the Missouri wild. I recall with amused pleasure the plates of food that began to make daily appearances in our office refrigerator when Kevin started working there. Ceramic dinner plates laden with wild game, a vegetable and a starch from the previous night's meal of squirrel, paddlefish or venison started crowding the space around the processed cheese slices and microwave lunches of other office inhabitants.

Nature's ability to help "reset his balance" is high on Kevin's list of reasons to hunt and be in the wild. "In this modern, digital era, a person can feel pretty disconnected from everything. When I get out in the woods, it doesn't take long to get the feeling that I could be living a thousand years ago—using what I have learned about animals and their behaviors, and putting into practice my familiarity with the outdoor environment and my skills as a hunter. There's a calming effect and intimacy from all of it that is very healing."

whet your appetite for the outdoors at MDC workshops

Want to try fishing, hunting, camping or other outdoor sports, but don't know how to get started? The Conservation Department sponsors *Discover Nature* programs designed to teach adults and children a variety of outdoor skills. Choose from courses in archery, hunting, canoeing, outdoor cooking, introduction to firearms, camping, fishing fundamentals, fly tying, map and compass, and shotgun shooting. For more information, visit *mdc. mo.gov/discover-nature*.

Discover Hunting programs are designed to be a bridge for those who have completed hunter-education training but still want some guidance and instruction. Mentored hunts and hands-on workshops build on the foundation of hunter education to create knowledgeable, responsible and confident hunters ready to go afield for their first actual hunts. For details, visit *mdc. mo.gov/hunting-trapping/ learn-hunt/discover-hunting*.

"I like to hunt for not only the meat, but the enjoyment of being out in the woods," says Mary Lyon, who hunts on her property in southern Boone County. She harvests only what she can eat and share with dinner guests.

"I like the idea of eating a local meat and harvesting it myself. I also like knowing what the animal has been eating and the areas in which it has roamed—things you don't always know when you get meat from other sources. It's a lean, healthful meat that complements other locally raised foods."

This is one of my favorite ways to use ground venison. Quick and easy, this recipe also is incredibly malleable, as I've mentioned in my herbs and spices note that follows. In a nutshell, kebabs are miniature Middle Eastern meatloaves on sticks. I love to tuck them into grilled pitas and top them with fresh heirloom cherry tomatoes and yogurt-cucumber dip. Lemony rice-shaped pasta and grilled peppers and eggplant round out the feast.

venison kebabs

Serves 4 to 6

1 pound ground venison
½ cup finely chopped onion
¼ cup finely chopped fresh parsley
¼ cup finely chopped fresh cilantro
4 garlic cloves, minced
1 teaspoon salt
¾ teaspoon coarsely ground black pepper
½ teaspoon paprika
   (or smoked Spanish paprika)
¾ teaspoon hot red pepper flakes
1 tablespoon extra-virgin olive oil

Pita bread

Equipment: 6 (10- or 12-inch-long) bamboo skewers
   (See *Soak Your Skewers* below.)
   Oiled baking sheet

Mix all ingredients together and chill for at least 3 hours or overnight. Remove skewers from water and shake off excess; firmly pack meat mixture around the skewers in 3-inch-long, 1-inch-thick links—two to a skewer.

Place skewers on the oiled baking sheet and carefully turn them to lightly coat the meat with oil. Remove skewers from the sheet carefully and place them on a grill heated to medium. Cook 10 to 15 minutes—carefully and gently turning them halfway through. A metal spatula gently pushed under the kebabs helps to turn them.

Serve sandwich style in freshly grilled pita bread. Top the kebabs with fresh, chopped tomatoes and *Tzatziki*. Accompany with *Lemony Orzo* and uncork your favorite red wine.

soak your skewers

Bamboo skewers are my choice for threading meat for satays or kebabs. Be sure to soak the skewers in water for at least 30 minutes (or more) to keep them from igniting on the grill. Metal skewers don't need to be soaked, of course, but they do get (and stay) very hot. Also, they often are bigger and tear the meat when threading in a way that the smaller bamboo ones don't.

suit yourself with seasonings

The herb-and-spice mixture can be adjusted to suit your palate when you are mixing all the ingredients together. For example, when I created this recipe, I first tried the mixture with less garlic, hot pepper flakes and salt. To test for seasoning, I made a 1-inch-round ball and cooked it in the microwave for a few seconds. If it tasted too bland, I kept experimenting until I had the desired amount of spiciness in the raw mixture. Once when I made these I didn't have cilantro on hand, so I used various other herbs from my garden including rosemary, oregano, chives, basil and thyme. I also threw in a few fennel seeds. So the herb and spice blend is not strict. You may want to try it this way the first time, then the next time use your own combination of fresh herbs and spices from your pantry.

lemony orzo   Serves 4 to 6

½ pound orzo (rice-shaped pasta)
1 tablespoon fresh lemon juice
Zest from ½ large lemon
2 tablespoons finely chopped fresh parsley
1 ounce feta cheese, crumbled into bite-sized chunks
Extra-virgin olive oil
Salt
Coarsely ground black pepper

Cook pasta, drain and toss with lemon juice, zest, parsley, cheese and a healthy drizzle of olive oil. Season to taste and serve immediately.

---

tzatziki   Makes 1 cup of dip

This cool and creamy yogurt-cucumber dip is perfect for slathering onto your hot venison kebabs. A ubiquitous appetizer/salad in Greece and the Middle East, it has many interpretations among cooks. Here is my quick and easy version.

1 small to medium cucumber (long, narrow, almost-seedless varieties work best)
1 cup plain yogurt
1 large garlic clove, minced
2 teaspoons extra-virgin olive oil
2 teaspoons lemon juice
1 tablespoon finely chopped fresh dill
1 teaspoon finely chopped fresh mint
Salt and freshly ground pepper to taste

Peel cucumber if it is not an Asian or almost-seedless variety. Remove seeds and dice or grate. Combine with rest of ingredients in a glass or ceramic dish and chill to allow flavors to blend. Serve as an accompaniment to venison kebabs.

Note: If you like a thicker version of this dip, strain both the yogurt and cucumbers separately through sieves to drain away liquid before combining with other ingredients.

Traditional Italian ragù—mellow, rich and complex—is quite different from the commercially jarred variety that has become familiar on supermarket shelves. Instead, the sauce is very meaty, with less tomato taste than is customary for Americans. This all-day sauce (traditionally made with beef) is delicious and worth every minute of your time. Make it on a cold winter's day when you have a few hours at your disposal to cook and do some household tasks. Most of the work is up front in an hour of chopping and prepping. After that, it's a matter of stirring the pot once in a while and waiting for liquid to evaporate. So put on your favorite music, assemble the sauce, and delight in the aromas coming from the pot.

venison ragù (Bolognese-style meat sauce)

Serves 14 to 18

⅓ cup vegetable oil

6 tablespoons butter

1¾ cups chopped onions

2¼ cups chopped celery

2¼ cups chopped carrots

2 pounds ground venison

¾ pound ground pork (or ¼ pound thick, smoky bacon (chopped coarsely) and ½ pound ground pork)

Salt and freshly ground black pepper

3½ cups milk

Whole nutmeg, freshly grated

3 cups dry white wine

2 28-ounce cans diced tomatoes, with their juice

Freshly grated Parmigiano-Reggiano cheese

Put oil, butter and onions in a large stockpot. Cook and stir over medium heat until onions becomes translucent. Add celery and carrots. Cook for a few minutes, stirring and coating the vegetables well. Add meat, several healthy pinches of salt and 9 or 10 grindings of pepper. Break the meat into small pieces with a wooden spoon and stir well. Cook until it has lost its raw color.

Add milk to the pot and simmer gently, stirring often, until it has bubbled away. Add a few gratings of nutmeg (about ⅓ teaspoon) and stir well. Add wine and simmer until it has evaporated. Add tomatoes and stir thoroughly to coat all ingredients well. When tomatoes start bubbling, turn the heat down to simmer. Cook, uncovered, for at least 3 hours and stir occasionally. Add ½ cup water whenever necessary to keep meat from sticking. When done, no water should be left. Taste and correct for salt and pepper.

Use sauce to layer lasagne or toss with cooked drained pasta. Serve with freshly grated cheese at the table.

big batch for many uses

This is a huge batch, but I had 2 pounds of ground venison to use, and I wasn't about to let any go to waste. With this batch I made fresh-spinach lasagne for dinner and froze the rest of the sauce. Two months later, I thawed the sauce and tossed it with dry pasta; it was delicious. Conchiglie (shells) or fusilli (corkscrews) are perfect for capturing bite-sized chunks of the sauce in their little cavities.

an adaptation from the master

This recipe was adapted from *Essentials of Classic Italian Cooking* by Marcella Hazan, with whom I studied in Bologna many years ago. Through her classes and cookbooks, Hazan did for Italian cooking in the United States what Julia Child did for French. I recommend her books to anyone with a serious interest in cooking Italian food.

I almost didn't include chili in this book because I figured everyone knows how to make it and has his or her own favorite version. However, sometimes I'm inspired to make even a familiar dish just because seeing a recipe somewhere is a reminder to do so. I figured other people might feel the same. As I flipped through an old chili-lovers' cookbook I found on my shelf, I was amazed to see the variety of things people put in their chili—chocolate, coffee, sour cream and vodka, among other things. Thick or thin, with cornbread or crackers, beans or not, chili seems to be Americans' favorite one-dish meal. I decided on a version based upon the memory of my mother's. We always had it with fresh carrots, celery and crackers on the side.

venison chili

Serves 4 to 6

1 large onion, chopped

4 garlic cloves, minced

3 tablespoons vegetable or extra-virgin olive oil

1 pound ground venison

1 to 1½ cups fresh and/or frozen roasted peppers, coarsely chopped

1 28-ounce can fire-roasted diced tomatoes

2 cups tomato juice

3 cups water

3 cups beef broth (organic, in aseptic package or can)

1 bay leaf

1½ teaspoons salt

1½ teaspoons freshly ground cumin

A few pinches of your best chile powder

A few pinches of smoked paprika

A few pinches of coarsely ground black pepper

A couple of pinches of oregano

1 to 1½ cups beans, freshly cooked or canned (pinto, navy or bean of your choice)

In a soup pot, sauté onion and garlic in oil until softened. Add venison, stirring until cooked through.

Add rest of ingredients, stir well and bring to a boil. Reduce to simmer and partially cover. Stir occasionally, and during the last half hour, add beans.

Total cooking time will vary, but I usually let the pot simmer for about 2 hours or until I can't resist the urge to ladle it into a bowl and eat.

clean out the freezer

Chili is a good dish in which to use the frozen bounty of your garden. I dug deep into my freezer when I made this, and found several of the ingredients—hot and sweet peppers, tomatoes and tomato juice.

"Food is the most primitive form of comfort."

—Sheila Graham

Almost every culture has a stuffed savory bun in its culinary heritage, and this is one of my favorites. It was passed on to me from Rainer Hochhalter, a childhood friend from High Hill, the mid-Missouri town where I grew up. His mother, Ilse (a native of Hamburg, Germany) made these sweet dinner rolls stuffed with the traditional ground beef, onion and cabbage. The venison, caraway seeds and garlic are my own variations.

venison bierocks (meat-stuffed buns)

Makes 24 buns

Dough

1 cup milk

½ cup sugar

1 teaspoon salt

½ cup vegetable oil

1 package yeast

1 cup lukewarm water

1 egg

6 cups flour (I like one-third whole wheat)

Filling

1 pound venison, ground

2 tablespoons butter

1¼ cups chopped onions

2 large garlic cloves, minced

5 cups cabbage, chopped
    (about half a good-sized head)

1½ teaspoons caraway seeds

2 teaspoons sugar

2 teaspoons vinegar

1¼ teaspoons salt

¾ teaspoon coarsely ground pepper

¼ cup water

2 teaspoons flour

Dijon, other good-quality mustard, or *Mustard Sauce* (See page 27.)

Make the dough

Scald milk; add sugar, salt and vegetable oil, then cool in large bowl. Dissolve yeast in lukewarm water in separate small bowl. Add to milk mixture and stir in beaten egg. Add 3 cups flour and mix until smooth. Work in remaining flour or enough to make an easily handled dough. Knead well (8 to 10 minutes). Place the ball of dough in an oiled bowl, turning to coat with oil. Cover and let rise in a warm place until doubled in bulk (1½ to 2 hours). Punch down and let rise again for 30 to 45 minutes.

Make the filling

Brown meat in a large sauté pan, drain and set aside in a bowl. Melt butter in same pan and sauté onions and garlic until soft. Remove from pan and add to the meat in the bowl. Add cabbage to the sauté pan along with the next six ingredients (through water). Cover pan and cook at a lively simmer for 10 to 12 minutes, stirring several times. Drain juices, add flour and stir well. Add meat, onions and garlic. Season to taste with more salt and pepper, if desired. Mix thoroughly and let cool.

Stuff the dough

Preheat oven to 350°F. Roll dough into a large square, about ¼-inch thick. Cut into 4-inch squares, and keep covered with a cloth as you work. Mound ¼ cup filling onto the middle of each square, bring opposite corners together and pinch seams firmly to form either a square or a circle, to your liking.

Set buns, with smooth side up, on 2 greased baking sheets and let rise about 30 minutes. Bake 15 to 20 minutes until nice and brown. Brush lightly with butter. Cut in halves, if you like, and slather with a good sturdy mustard or the fabulous mustard sauce on the adjacent page.

the bun that likes to travel

These luscious little pocket pastries are great travel companions; stick a few in your pack when hiking or going on a picnic. They're also welcome on the groaning boards at all kinds of fall and winter parties, especially Oktoberfest.

mustard sauce Makes 4 to 5 small (4-ounce) jars of mustard sauce

Bierocks are fabulous when slathered with this mustard sauce, and so are ham sandwiches and just about anything else. Friend Barbara Leslie contributed the recipe. She adapted it from the "Boone Docs" cookbook, a Boone County recipe collection published in the 1970s. By the way, Barb says no substitutes are allowed for Colman's, the brand of mustard also preferred by the British Royal Family.

1 cup vinegar (cider, white or wine)
1 cup (4 ounces) Colman's English mustard powder
2 eggs
½ teaspoon salt
1 cup sugar
Dill weed (optional)

Mix vinegar and mustard powder together, cover and allow to stand overnight. Beat eggs well in a separate bowl; stir in salt and sugar. Combine mustard and egg mixtures and blend well. Pour into the top of a double boiler and cook until the mixture is the consistency of a medium-thin sauce, whisking often as it cooks. Keep in mind that the sauce will thicken, also, as it cools. Pour into jars and cover with lids. The sauce improves with age and keeps in the refrigerator indefinitely. It makes a highly coveted gift for mustard lovers, too.

This is a wonderful dish to make in the late summer or early fall, when your garden is on the wane, but still producing a small bounty of eggplants, peppers and tomatoes. This recipe is an adaptation of the classic Greek dish, which often is made with ground lamb. Moussaka has a few steps to it, so plan on the good part of an afternoon to put it together. Alternatively, to save time on serving day, you may make the meat sauce the day before. I promise that your labors will be richly rewarded when you bite into one of the most blissful marriages ever of vegetables, meat and spices. Crowned with a glorious cheesy white sauce, moussaka is an ideal calorie splurge every so often! It also keeps for several days and seems to improve with age, so make it a day or two in advance and reheat it if you choose.

venison moussaka

Serves 6 to 8

Meat mixture

5 tablespoons extra-virgin olive oil

3 sweet, medium red bell peppers, cut into 1-inch pieces

1½ pounds ground venison

1 medium onion, coarsely chopped

2 teaspoons minced garlic

½ cup dry red wine

3 cups chopped plum tomatoes (about 1½ pounds)

2 tablespoons tomato paste

1 teaspoon cinnamon

½ teaspoon allspice

1 teaspoon salt

½ teaspoon coarsely ground pepper

1 bay leaf

¼ cup chopped fresh Italian parsley

½ teaspoon chopped fresh oregano

2 eggs separated (save yolks for sauce)

½ cup breadcrumbs

2½ pounds eggplants (about 3 medium), cut lengthwise into ⅓-inch-thick slices

White sauce

6 tablespoons butter

6 tablespoons flour

3 cups milk

White pepper (preferably freshly ground)

Nutmeg, freshly grated

1 cup grated Pecorino Romano cheese

Prepare the meat mixture

Heat 2 tablespoons olive oil in large sauté pan over medium-high heat. Add peppers and sauté until tender, about 8 minutes. Transfer peppers to a bowl and heat 3 tablespoons oil in same skillet over medium-high heat. Add venison and sauté until cooked through, breaking up with back of spoon, about 5 minutes. Add onion and garlic and sauté until tender, about 5 minutes. Add wine and cook 2 minutes. Stir in tomatoes, paste and next seven ingredients (through oregano). Cover and simmer until sauce is very thick, stirring occasionally, about 30 minutes. Remove from heat and let cool. Remove bay leaf, add egg whites and 2 tablespoons breadcrumbs. Mix well.

> "A significant part of the pleasure of eating is in one's accurate consciousness of the lives and the world from which food comes." —Wendell Berry

Prepare the eggplant

While the meat mixture cools, line a large baking sheet with foil. Arrange eggplant slices in layers on the baking sheet, sprinkling each layer with salt. Let stand at room temperature 30 minutes.

Preheat broiler. Line another large baking sheet with foil. Pat eggplant slices dry with paper towels. Arrange some of the slices in a single layer on the second baking sheet. Brush each slice lightly with olive oil on both sides. Broil about 3 minutes per side. Transfer to a platter, and repeat with remaining eggplant.

Make the white sauce

In a heavy saucepan, melt the butter but don't let it brown. Using a wire whisk, stir in flour. Cook, stirring for 1 to 2 minutes over low heat. Gradually stir in the milk, whisking all the while. At the same time, gently increase the heat until the mixture comes to a boil. Stir steadily until it is a smooth sauce. Mix in white pepper and a few gratings of nutmeg. Remove from heat and let the sauce cool for a few minutes. Gently whisk in beaten egg yolks. The sauce should be thicker than gravy, but thinner than pudding. If it still needs to thicken, return to low heat and whisk gently until it reaches the right consistency.

Assemble the moussaka

Preheat oven to 350°F. Coat a 12- by 9- by 2-inch baking dish with olive oil. Sprinkle bottom of the dish with remaining breadcrumbs. Layer half the eggplant slices atop the breadcrumbs. Cover completely with half the meat mixture, spreading evenly with a spatula. Arrange sautéed peppers over meat. Sprinkle with half the cheese. Layer the remaining eggplant over cheese, then spoon on the remainder of the meat mixture. Top with white sauce and sprinkle with remaining cheese. Bake 40 to 45 minutes or until the top turns golden in color. Remove from the oven to a rack and allow to cool for 10 to 15 minutes. Cut into squares and serve.

Accompany with crusty bread and a salad of fresh mixed fall greens, tart sliced apple and toasted pecans. Your favorite dry, red wine completes the meal.

Marcia Vanderlip—food editor for the *Columbia Daily Tribune*—and her husband, Scott Cairns, have a passion for Greece and its cuisine. Inspired by both a recent visit to the country and the bountiful produce on display at the Columbia Farmers Market one August morning, they came up with this version of the popular Greek dish. It has much in common with moussaka, but the pasta gives it an extra layer of richness. Marcia's original recipe calls for lamb, but venison works beautifully.

farmers market venison pastitsio

Serves 8 to 12

Meat mixture

2 tablespoons extra-virgin olive oil

2 pounds ground venison

1 medium onion, chopped

½ cup dry white wine

2 large heirloom tomatoes, blanched, peeled, seeded and puréed

2 tablespoons chopped fresh parsley

½ teaspoon allspice

1 teaspoon cinnamon

Salt and freshly ground black pepper to taste

1 pound fresh penne pasta

2 tablespoons breadcrumbs

¼ cup unsalted butter

2 medium zucchini, julienned

2 medium summer squash, julienned

4 egg whites (reserve the yolks for béchamel sauce)

1½ cups grated Pecorino Romano cheese

1 medium eggplant, sliced, salted, set between paper towels for 10 minutes and rinsed

Béchamel sauce

½ cup unsalted butter

½ cup flour

2 cups milk, warmed

4 egg yolks, beaten lightly

Pinch of ground nutmeg

½ pound sliced oyster mushrooms, lightly sautéed in a dab of butter

Begin with the meat

Heat olive oil in a large sauté pan. Add venison and cook over medium-high heat until pink color disappears, about 5 minutes. Add onion and cook until translucent, about 5 minutes more.

Add wine, puréed tomatoes, parsley, allspice, cinnamon, salt and pepper, and allow sauce to simmer and thicken over medium low heat for 20 minutes. While sauce is simmering, put water on to boil for pasta. Cook fresh pasta until slightly underdone (about 3 minutes). Drain pasta in colander under cold water to stop cooking.

Stir breadcrumbs into meat sauce to absorb excess liquid. Remove from heat.

Melt ¼ cup butter in pasta pot and stir in the julienned veggies. Return cooked pasta to the pot. Stir in beaten egg whites and 1 cup of cheese; toss lightly, being careful not to break the noodles.

Brush the bottom and sides of a lasagna pan with olive oil. Layer the bottom with the sliced eggplant and cover with half of the pasta mix; press down so that the pasta layer is somewhat flattened. Add the meat sauce in an even layer over the pasta. Top with remaining pasta mix and flatten top layer evenly with the back of a spatula.

Preheat the oven to 350°F while you prepare the béchamel sauce.

Make the béchamel sauce

Melt butter in a saucepan over low heat. Using a whisk, add flour to melted butter, whisking continuously to make a smooth paste or roux. Allow the flour-butter mixture to cook for a minute, but do not allow it to brown.

Add milk to mixture in a steady stream, whisking continuously. Simmer over low heat until it thickens, but does not boil.

Remove from heat for a minute, then stir in egg yolks and nutmeg. Béchamel should be thicker than gravy, but not as thick as pudding. If sauce still needs to thicken, return to very low heat and continue to stir. When the sauce reaches the right consistency, fold the mushrooms in and pour over the pasta layer, making sure to pour sauce down into the corners, as well. Sprinkle with remaining ½ cup cheese. Bake approximately 45 minutes or until the top is a nice golden color.

MARCIA VANDERLIP

31

Venison adapts well to this rustic British favorite, which usually is made with beef or lamb. Sweet potatoes put a sweeter twist on the traditional white-potato topping.

venison shepherd's pie
with sweet potatoes

Serves 6

Topping
2½ pounds sweet potatoes, peeled, cut into 2-inch pieces
1 medium russet potato, peeled, cut into 2-inch pieces
2 tablespoons butter
2 tablespoons pure maple syrup

Spice blend
¼ teaspoon whole coriander
¼ teaspoon whole cumin
¼ teaspoon whole fenugreek
¼ teaspoon whole cardamom seeds
¼ teaspoon whole mustard seeds
¼ teaspoon whole fennel seeds
¼ teaspoon whole cloves
1½ teaspoons cayenne pepper
1 teaspoon turmeric
½ teaspoon cinnamon
1 teaspoon salt

Meat mixture
1½ pounds ground venison
2 cups chopped onions
5 large garlic cloves, minced
3 tablespoons extra-virgin olive oil
¾ cup frozen peas
¾ cup frozen corn kernels
½ cup half and half or cream
1 large egg, lightly beaten

Steam potatoes in double boiler until tender, about 25 minutes. Drain water from bottom pan and pour in potatoes. Add butter and syrup. Season to taste with salt and pepper. Mash mixture until smooth.

Grind whole spices in an electric grinder or mortar and pestle, then mix with cayenne pepper, turmeric, cinnamon and salt. In a large bowl, mix venison with spice blend, onions and garlic.

Preheat oven to 350°F. Butter 9- by 12-inch glass or ceramic baking dish. Heat olive oil in a large sauté pan and cook meat mixture until brown and cooked through, turning and breaking up large pieces with the back of a spoon. Season to taste with salt and pepper, and add more cayenne if you desire a hotter taste. Let meat mixture cool, then mix in peas, corn, half and half, and egg.

Transfer meat mixture to the prepared baking dish. Spoon a smooth layer of mashed potatoes over the top. Bake until heated through and potatoes begin to brown around edges, about 45 minutes. Place under the broiler for a couple of minutes to brown top. Let stand 5 minutes before serving.

Serve with a fresh green salad that has been tossed with a vinaigrette, orange sections, avocado and almonds. A Shiraz or Zinfandel pairs well with the bold spices in this dish.

Note: This dish can be prepared 1 day ahead, then covered and refrigerated for later use. You'll need to increase the baking time by about 15 minutes if you put it into the oven cold.

One spring evening after gardening all day until dark, I was famished and weary, but didn't have anything prepared that would do for supper. I perused the contents of the refrigerator and came up with a quick little dish that hit the spot. Using leftovers creatively is a challenge that enthuses me, but it helps to have really tasty scraps on hand. I was fortunate to find a few slices of venison summer sausage tucked away behind some containers. Leftover from a recent potluck, the sausage was from a friend—Lisa Guillory—who had harvested the deer the previous fall. The garlic greens, onion and kale had been procured from my weekly stop at the farmers market, and the herbs were from my garden. I encourage you to create your own version, using your favorite vegetables, herbs and cheese.

venison sausage frittata

Serves 2 to 4

3 fresh asparagus spears

½ cup chopped onion

2 tablespoons extra-virgin olive oil

6 eggs

Salt and freshly ground pepper

⅔ cup freshly grated
Parmigiano-Reggiano cheese

1 cup venison sausage, cut into
bite-sized pieces

2 tablespoons finely chopped fresh
herbs (basil, parsley, chives, thyme)

2 tablespoons chopped green garlic
(optional)

1 cup chopped fresh spinach,
kale or chard

2 tablespoons butter

Steam asparagus until tender but firm to the bite. Plunge into ice water for a few seconds to stop the cooking. Drain and set aside to cool, then cut into ½-inch lengths.

Sauté onion in oil until soft. Remove from pan and set aside.

Beat the eggs in a bowl until well-blended and add the asparagus, onion, a couple of pinches of salt and a few grindings of pepper. Add the rest of the ingredients (except butter) and mix well.

Turn on your broiler. A frittata is cooked on both sides, and running it under a broiler works well.

Melt the butter in a 10-inch cast-iron skillet over medium heat. As soon as it begins to foam, pour in the egg mixture and stir with a fork while pouring out of the bowl. Turn the heat to medium-low. When the eggs on bottom have set and thickened, but the eggs on top are still runny, put the skillet under the broiler for a few seconds. Don't take your eyes off the skillet, because the contents will cook quickly (in a minute or less). Take the frittata out at the first hint of browning.

Loosen it with a spatula, slide onto a plate, and cut into wedges. Serve with lightly dressed fresh lettuce and a wedge of fresh bread. A glass of Sauvignon Blanc complements nicely.

versatile, and good the next day, too

This dish is large enough for two hearty meals or four small ones. I took my leftovers to the office for lunch the next day and shared with a co-worker. I love a frittata at room temperature as much as I do hot out of the skillet. It also makes a great sandwich, picnic item or contribution to an appetizer platter.

the venison prosciutto challenge
—can anybody spare a ham?

During a trip to Italy amidst the process of writing this cookbook, I had the pleasure of sampling venison prosciutto in a small Alpine village. I've packed away a lot of traditional prosciutto (Italian cured ham, shown below) in my time, but never had encountered a venison version. When I inquired, the owner of the restaurant told me it was a traditional cured meat of the area. Served as an appetizer—paper thin, delicate and complex at the same time—it was divine. A local red-currant mostarda, an Italian condiment, accompanied it.

I couldn't stop thinking about whether or not any experienced Missouri deer hunters (especially those who make venison sausage) had ever attempted the art of prosciutto making here. When I returned to Missouri, I checked with a few seasoned hunters who said they weren't aware of anyone who was doing it, but they sure would like to try some. Herein lies the challenge.

Even though the art of making prosciutto is steeped in a 2,000-year-old tradition of hams made under very specific conditions, the Italians are not alone in the art of curing hindquarters. Missourians have been at it a little while themselves, and consistently turn out some fine hams. Consequently, I'm suggesting that a few deer hunters should cross paths with those who cure hams to see if a venison prosciutto tradition could be born here.

Coming to the aid of this challenge is Brook Harlan, a culinary arts instructor at the Columbia Area Career Center. An old hand at curing meats himself, Brook also instructs his students in the art. Every semester they turn out tasty prosciutto, pancetta, andouille and other pork products. Brook says he would welcome a few deer hindquarters with which to do a venison prosciutto experiment with his students. Deer hunters willing to "lend a ham" should contact Brook at *BHarlan@columbia.k12.mo.us* for more details.

35

I love to make this Thai-inspired venison salad when I have a package of meat scraps to use. The marinade goes together quickly and the ingredients are flexible. I use different combinations of vegetables, depending upon what I have on hand or what is in season. It's a perfect hot-weather dish to serve outdoors.

Thai venison salad

Serves 4 as a light meal

1 pound venison scrap or stir-fry pieces
2 teaspoons vegetable oil

1 cup fresh lime juice (about 6 good-sized limes)
¼ cup Thai fish sauce, or to taste
2 teaspoons brown sugar (or to taste)
4 large garlic cloves, minced
1 teaspoon coarsely ground black pepper
4 or 5 small, fresh red or green chiles
    (Thai, serrano or jalapeno), minced

1 medium Asian (seedless) cucumber
1 large sweet red pepper, sliced diagonally
2 carrots, sliced diagonally
2 cups fresh bean sprouts
4 green onions, thinly sliced
½ cup thinly sliced red onion
½ cup coarsely chopped fresh cilantro
4 tablespoons chopped fresh mint

4 to 6 Romaine lettuce leaves
⅓ cup toasted peanuts, chopped coarsely

Toasted sesame oil
Cooked white rice

Equipment: Bamboo skewers if you are starting with small pieces of meat

Heat grill to medium. If you have a 1-pound piece of venison, cut into two pieces, brush with vegetable oil, and grill until desired doneness. Cut meat across the grain into thin, bite-sized pieces (approximately 1-inch squares, ¼ inch thick). If you have scraps to use, cut larger ones across the grain into bite-sized strips and thread all the pieces on skewers that have been soaked in water for at least a half hour prior to grilling. Brush skewered meat well with vegetable oil before placing on grill. Cook 10 to 12 minutes (or until desired doneness), turning often. Make sure the meat gets just a little crispy on the outside.

Blend lime juice, fish sauce, sugar, garlic and pepper together— along with 2 heaping teaspoons of the minced hot chiles (save the rest to pass at the table). Pour half of the marinade into a large bowl (reserving the rest for the table). Add venison to the bowl. Stir and refrigerate 2 hours.

Meanwhile, prepare the rest of the ingredients. Score the cucumber lengthwise with tines of a fork. Cut the cucumber in half lengthwise, scoop out any seeds, and cut it diagonally into thin slices. Cut red pepper into bite-sized strips. Refrigerate vegetables until ready to assemble the dish.

Remove venison from refrigerator 15 minutes prior to serving. Toss sweet red pepper, carrots, sprouts, onions, cilantro and mint into the bowl with venison and marinade. Blend well. Arrange lettuce leaves on serving platter. Mound venison salad in center. Surround with cucumber slices and garnish with peanuts.

Set the table with small dishes of minced fresh hot chiles, the remaining marinade and sesame oil, if you choose. Accompany with cold watermelon slices. Dark beer complements the salad's spicy flavors. If you don't serve the salad with hot rice, then *Coconut Sticky Rice with Mango* (page 38) would be a delightful dessert.

I always have adored coconut and mango separately. However, after I had my first taste of this light dessert at a Thai restaurant many years ago, I decided the fruits were meant to be together. The following proportions yield a subtle coconut flavor. You may find that you prefer a stronger and sweeter dessert. If so, increase the amount of coconut milk and brown sugar. A dead-ripe mango, of course, is requisite for making the dish outstanding.

coconut sticky rice with mango

Serves 6

2 cups short-grained (sushi) white rice
2 cups water
1 cup light coconut milk
⅓ cup brown sugar
Pinch of salt
Pinch of cinnamon
1 large ripe fresh mango
2 teaspoons black sesame seeds

Rinse rice thoroughly (until water runs almost clear) in a fine-mesh strainer.

Combine in saucepan with 2 cups water and bring to a boil. Let boil for 1 minute, then reduce heat to simmer and cover pan tightly with lid. Cook 20 minutes and remove from heat.

Heat coconut milk and sugar until sugar dissolves.

Turn hot rice out into a bowl. Pour milk, sugar, salt and cinnamon over the rice. Stir well and adjust seasonings, if needed. Let mixture come to room temperature.

Serve in individual bowls with slices of mango. Sprinkle with sesame seeds.

Green-chile stew is one of my favorite fireside comfort foods—not one that I grew up with, however. Since my first visit to northern New Mexico many years ago, that state's signature dish calls to me on snowy Missouri nights. It is traditionally made with beef or pork in the Southwest, but venison also does it justice. Several containers of New Mexican chopped green chiles were in my freezer from a recent trip, so I pulled out a couple to try in this recipe. After the first taste, I congratulated myself for having had the foresight to bring them home with me. Yum!

venison green-chile stew

Makes about 10 cups of stew

2 pounds venison, cut into ½-inch cubes

¼ cup vegetable oil

2 medium onions, diced

6 large garlic cloves, minced

2 pounds potatoes, cut in ½-inch cubes

1 tablespoon salt

6 cups chicken broth

3 cups chopped fire-roasted mild or hot green chiles, preferably New Mexican

2 sweet or hot fresh peppers, minced (See *Pick a Pepper*.)

Several pinches of freshly ground black pepper

¼ cup chopped fresh cilantro

Whole wheat- or white-flour tortillas

In a large, heavy saucepan, cook the venison in oil over medium heat until browned and most of the liquid has evaporated. Stir in onions and garlic and cook for 3 or 4 minutes. Add potatoes, salt and broth. Bring contents to a boil. Reduce to a simmer and cook uncovered for an hour.

Add the chiles, fresh peppers and black pepper, and cook 1 hour or more until the venison is tender and the stew is of desired consistency.

Ladle into soup bowls and sprinkle with cilantro. Accompany with warm tortillas for dipping into or stuffing with the stew.

pick a pepper

You may use any kind of fresh or frozen pepper for the minced peppers. I have friends who grow a large variety of heirloom peppers every summer on their farm in Shannon County. They preserve plenty for winter by chopping them finely in a food processor and freezing the pulp flat in large freezer bags. Being a beneficiary of many of their fresh peppers, I've started doing the same. It works great for recipes such as green-chile stew. I pulled out a freezer bag and pinched off 2 or 3 tablespoons of puréed mixed hot and sweet peppers and threw them into the pan with the chiles.

make it hotter or milder

Only your taste buds can decide how much hot pepper you want to add. If you use mostly mild green chiles, then you'll want to add fresh hot peppers for extra kick. I like a ratio of about two-thirds mild and one-third hot New Mexican green chiles to begin with. Then, upon tasting, if I decide it needs more punch, I throw in the fresh hot peppers. If you find the stew too spicy, add extra broth and a little water to dilute the heat.

This is my version of bulgogi, a Korean dish that has many interpretations. With a few minutes of advance work earlier in the day, you can throw this together in no time right before eating. It's a good choice for a hot, summer evening when grilling and light eating are on your mind. I like to eat this as a salad, but alternatively, you may tuck the meat, rice and accompaniments into a big leaf of lettuce and eat taco style.

Korean barbecued venison

1 pound venison (scrap or stir-fry pieces work well)

Marinade

2 tablespoons soy sauce

2 teaspoons toasted sesame oil

2 teaspoons minced garlic

1 teaspoon minced fresh ginger root (peeled)

2 tablespoons brown sugar

1 tablespoon mirin (rice wine)

Dash of freshly ground coarse black pepper

Juice from ½ lime

Dipping sauce

4 tablespoons red miso (soybean paste)

2 tablespoons minced garlic

1 tablespoon minced fresh ginger root (peeled)

2 tablespoons red-pepper sauce, such as Tabasco

4 teaspoons vegetable oil

1 teaspoon toasted sesame oil

¼ cup water

Accompaniments

4 cups cooked short- or medium-grained rice

12 leaves of red-leaf or mixed red and green lettuces

2 cups mung bean sprouts

½ cup cilantro, loosely packed

½ cup fresh mint, loosely packed

1 fresh green hot pepper, finely chopped (optional)

1½ cups kim chee (purchased or prepared in advance)

Equipment: 4 long bamboo skewers

Cut the venison into ¼-inch-thick slices; then cut each into 1- by 1-inch pieces. Mix together marinade ingredients in a bowl and then add venison pieces. Toss thoroughly. Marinate in refrigerator 4 to 5 hours.

Mix together dipping-sauce ingredients in a small saucepan that later will be heated as the meat cooks. If mixed ahead of time, refrigerate until ready to heat.

About 1 hour before you are ready to eat, soak bamboo skewers in water (to moisten them so they won't burn on the grill) and prepare the accompaniments. After you put the rice on to cook, wash and dry lettuces and bean sprouts. Coarsely chop cilantro and mint, and mince hot pepper.

Thread the meat on the skewers and heat dipping sauce over low heat until hot. Sometimes, to save a step, I put the saucepan on the grill as the meat cooks, since a heat source is already available. However, the higher heat means that it must be stirred often and will need a lot less cooking time, so take care not to let it boil away.

Grill meat for a few minutes over hot fire, turning once. Remove meat when it's done to your liking. Slide meat off skewers with a fork.

dishing it up

On individual serving plates, place a shallow bed of lettuces. Spoon hot rice on top, and meat on top of that. Sprinkle with bean sprouts, cilantro, mint and hot pepper. Add a spoonful of kim chee. Pass dipping sauce so each person may use as desired. Alternatively, sometimes I toss grilled meat into dipping sauce before I place atop rice. This assures meat is coated evenly.

A dark beer is my beverage of choice with this dish. However, a Malbec also holds up well against the spicy flavors.

kim chee—a Korean national treasure

Kim chee—Korean pickled vegetable (most commonly, cabbage)—is an optional accompaniment to the bulgogi. It enhances the meat, however, with another tasty "layer" of crunch and spice. Officially designated a national treasure in South Korea, kim chee is said to have more than 160 documented variations there.

41

This is a dish that has as much going for it in the presentation department as it does in taste. When you bring this hearty and delicious stew to the table in its beautiful orange-orb container, your unsuspecting dinner guests will be impressed! I made this dish in early February from a Cinderella pumpkin I had purchased more than three months earlier at the farmers market. It had been adorning my kitchen since Halloween, and I needed to reclaim the counter space. Holding this stew was a stunning finale for the beautiful pumpkin.

venison in a pumpkin

Serves 8

1 10- to 12-pound pumpkin with stem

3 tablespoons vegetable oil

2 pounds venison stew meat, cut in 1-inch cubes

1 cup water

2 cups organic, low-sodium beef broth

¾ cup unsweetened coconut

⅓ cup dried apricots, chopped

2 large russet potatoes, cubed

2 medium sweet potatoes, cubed

4 carrots, cubed

1 large fresh sweet pepper (or combination of sweet and hot peppers), chopped in bite-sized pieces

1 teaspoon hot-pepper flakes (optional)

4 garlic cloves, minced

1 onion, chopped

2 teaspoons salt

Large pinch freshly ground black pepper

1 15-ounce can diced tomatoes

Wash pumpkin, cut off top and set aside, leaving a hole large enough from which to ladle stew after it has baked. Remove seeds and pulp. Place pumpkin in a large baking pan and set aside.

Heat 2 tablespoons oil in a large saucepan over medium-high heat. Place venison in the pan and cook until browned. Mix in the water, 1 cup of broth and remaining ingredients except tomatoes. Bring to a boil, then reduce heat, cover and simmer 2 hours, stirring occasionally.

Preheat oven to 325°F. Stir tomatoes and remaining cup of broth into the stew mixture. Wet pumpkin stem and wrap it with aluminum foil. Fill pumpkin with stew and fit the top back onto the pumpkin. Brush outside of the pumpkin with remaining tablespoon of oil. Bake 2 hours or until tender. Serve the stew from the pumpkin, scraping out some of the pumpkin meat with each serving. Accompany with dense, crusty French bread.

"Dining is and always was a great artistic opportunity."

—Frank Lloyd Wright

This particular Moroccan-inspired combination of ingredients is one I love with lamb. However, once I tried it with venison, a new favorite was born. The slow-cooked meat becomes fork tender as it simmers in the spicy, rich tomato sauce redolent of preserved lemon.

Moroccan spiced-braised venison

3 tablespoons extra-virgin olive oil

2 pounds venison round steak

Salt and coarsely ground pepper

1 teaspoon cardamom seeds

1 teaspoon cumin seeds

1 lemon, cut thinly into 8 to 10 slices

4 medium garlic cloves, sliced

1 medium onion, chopped

1 4-ounce jar chopped pimentos or 1 red bell pepper

1 tablespoon dried pepper flakes (preferably ancho)

½ cup prunes, pitted

1 cup chicken stock

1 15-ounce can diced tomatoes

In a 4-quart cast-iron pot, heat olive oil over medium heat. Salt and pepper steaks on both sides and add to hot oil. After first side is browned, turn over and add cardamom and cumin seeds to the oil around meat, and stir to heat seeds thoroughly. Add lemon, garlic, onion and pimentos and stir. Cook until onion is softened. Add pepper flakes, prunes, stock and tomatoes. Turn meat over, stir thoroughly and cover with lid. Simmer atop burner for 2 to 3 hours until meat is tender.

Place meat on a heated platter and cover. Skim fat from pot and bring contents to a boil to reduce liquids. Season to taste and pour over venison.

Serve with couscous or saffron rice and your favorite bold red wine.

I use this quick spice-rub treatment for pork loin, and decided it would complement a venison loin just as deliciously. I had been given a basket of fresh red plums one late-August day, several hours before I had planned to make the loin dish. I immediately thought I would turn the fruit into a jelly or tart, but serendipity took over. As soon as I begin to think about how the plums might play up the venison, their fate transformed in my imaginings to a beautiful scarlet pool of sauce surrounding the loin. If you don't have plums, however, don't fret. The venison is great without it.

spice-roasted venison loin
with plum sauce

Serves 2 to 4

1 venison loin (about 1 pound)

1 teaspoon salt

¾ teaspoon thyme

½ teaspoon cinnamon, freshly ground

½ teaspoon black pepper, coarsely ground

⅛ teaspoon nutmeg, freshly grated

⅛ teaspoon cloves, freshly ground

½ teaspoon cumin, freshly ground

2 fat garlic cloves, minced

½ cup chicken broth (organic, low-sodium)

Plum sauce

3 cups Missouri plums

3 to 6 tablespoons sugar (add more sugar
   if plums are tart; less if they are sweet)

Prepare the venison

Place loin in baking pan just large enough to accommodate it and set aside. Mix the next eight ingredients (everything except the broth) together in a small bowl; rub into the loin, covering the meat thoroughly. Cover and refrigerate at least 4 hours—overnight is better.

Add chicken broth to the pan and place pan on grill. Close grill cover and cook over medium-high heat 30 to 45 minutes, depending on desired doneness. Baste several times during cooking and turn once midway through.

Place the loin on a platter and slice, drizzle with pan juices, and surround with plum sauce. Garnish with fresh rosemary sprigs and plums.

Plum sauce

Simmer plums, sugar and 3 tablespoons water together in a covered pan for 20 minutes. Stir occasionally. Put plums in a food mill or sieve, and press through the pulp; discard skins and pits. Makes ½ to ¾ cup sauce.

a spicy note

I like to grind my own spices because I think the flavors are much more pronounced and fresh tasting than pre-ground spices. If you have an electric coffee grinder or a mortar and pestle, it takes very little time to grind spices, especially in small quantities.

braised rabbit
with fire-roasted tomatoes on polenta

Rabbit in sauce

2 medium rabbits

Salt and freshly cracked black pepper

6 tablespoons extra-virgin olive oil

8 garlic cloves, coarsely chopped

1 28-ounce can fire-roasted diced tomatoes

1 cup dry red wine

A few sprigs of fresh thyme

A few sprigs of fresh rosemary

Polenta

7 cups water

1 tablespoon salt

1⅔ cups coarsely ground yellow cornmeal

---

good eating and exercise

Don't let the long stirring time deter you from trying polenta in its many glorious guises. Aside from being economical and delicious, it will build muscles in your arms!

Cook the rabbit

Cut each rabbit into 4 or 5 pieces and season with salt and pepper. Heat oil in a sauté pan large enough to accommodate all the pieces. Add meat to pan and sauté on medium-high heat until the pieces are golden brown on both sides, turning them several times and gently shaking the pan while cooking. Allow 15 to 20 minutes for meat to brown nicely.

Add garlic to pan; stir and shake pan gently, coating the rabbit pieces with garlic. Cook briefly—about 1 minute. Stir in tomatoes, wine, ½ cup water and bring to a boil. Reduce heat to simmer, cover pan, and cook for about 1 hour. While the rabbit is cooking, make the polenta.

When rabbit is tender, remover from pan and set aside. Stir herbs into sauce and simmer until the sauce begins to thicken. Place rabbit back in pan to heat. Season to taste with salt and pepper.

Surround the polenta with rabbit pieces and sauce. Accompany with fresh asparagus in spring or sautéed kale in the fall or winter. A Missouri Norton is a good wine match for this robust dish.

Make the polenta

Bring water to a boil in a large, heavy saucepan. Add salt and keep the water boiling at a medium-high heat. Add the cornmeal very slowly in a thin stream. Stir constantly with a whisk as you are adding the cornmeal; make sure water keeps boiling, as well.

Once all the cornmeal has been added, start stirring with a wooden spoon. Again, keep the stirring constant and thorough, making sure the cornmeal on the sides of the pan gets well incorporated into the stirring. Continue to stir for 35 to 45 minutes.

The cornmeal becomes polenta when it forms a mass that pulls away from the sides of the pot. It should be thick at this point. Mound immediately into the center of a serving platter that is large enough to also accommodate the rabbit and sauce.

cornmeal and water—a beautiful marriage

The combination of two simple ingredients—cornmeal and water—results in polenta and some of the most wonderful dishes known to humankind. I have been delighted that, in recent years, polenta has become popular at restaurants throughout the United States. A longtime peasant staple in northern Italy, it remains well loved there today and enhances many meat and fish dishes. I love the versatility that is inherent in its many preparation styles. It is outstanding as a creamy, one-dish meal when butter and cheese are melted into it when it is still soft. It provides a delicious bed for the meat and juices of braised, stewed or roasted venison, quail, rabbit and fish. When allowed to cool, polenta can be sliced and grilled or baked. It also can be cut into sticks or wedges and fried.

One of my favorite childhood dishes was "fried mush," which my brother and I begged our mother to make on snowy weekend mornings. Mom would stir white cornmeal into boiling water, and when it cooked into a thickened porridge (polenta, but we didn't call it that), she poured it into a rectangular pan to cool. She chilled the porridge overnight, then cut it into a dozen or so pieces the next morning, dipped them in flour, and fried them in butter. We'd eat them with maple syrup, savoring the crispy outsides and soft insides.

rabbit rolled in mustard sauce

2 rabbits (about a pound each)
Salt and coarsely ground black pepper
2 tablespoons vegetable oil
1 medium onion, finely chopped
3 garlic cloves, minced
3 sprigs fresh thyme, leaves stripped
    from stems
2 tablespoons unsalted butter
1¼ cups dry white wine
2 cups chicken broth
4 tablespoons Dijon mustard
1 teaspoon cornstarch
2 tablespoons chopped fresh parsley leaves

Cut each rabbit into pieces and pat dry; season liberally with salt and pepper. In a large cast-iron skillet, heat oil over moderate heat, and brown rabbit on all sides. Remove from skillet and set aside.

Preheat oven to 350°F. Add 1 tablespoon butter to skillet, and melt over low heat, stirring up browned rabbit bits. Stir in onion, garlic and thyme, and cook until onion is soft. Add wine and boil until liquid is reduced by half. Return rabbit to skillet and add chicken broth. Place skillet uncovered into oven. Turn pieces occasionally and cook 45 minutes to 1 hour or until fork tender.

Remove rabbit from skillet and boil sauce over burner until reduced to 2 cups if cooking in oven hasn't reduced it that much already. In a small bowl stir together ⅓ cup sauce and mustard and whisk mixture back into sauce. Stir cornstarch into 1 tablespoon cold water and whisk into sauce. Simmer sauce, whisking, until thickened. Whisk in remaining tablespoon of butter, parsley, and salt and pepper to taste. Add rabbit to skillet and cook over low heat, turning to coat with sauce.

Mashed potatoes and sautéed collard greens or kale are good companions to the rabbit.

"I like to know the history of a food and of the place that it comes from; I like to imagine the hands of the people who grew it, transported it, processed it, and cooked it before it was served to me."

—Carlo Petrini

"Several things make the squirrel a great game animal," says squirrel aficionado Kevin Lohraff. "Squirrels are everywhere and accessible to just about everyone. The hunting season for them is long, so there is a lot of opportunity, and you don't need lots of expensive equipment. It's a beautiful thing to be able to walk out to the local woods in the morning and get your evening meal."

Kevin talks about his favorite ways to eat squirrels:

fried squirrel
with mashed potatoes and gravy

Nothing beats the smell of squirrel being fried in the skillet; it fills up the kitchen with a wonderful aroma. I cut a few squirrels in pieces and boil them for 1½ to 3 hours (older squirrels need to cook longer) until just before the meat begins to fall off the bones. I roll the pieces in seasoned flour the way I do for fried chicken, and then fry them in the skillet. Of course, I always make lots of mashed potatoes and gravy to eat with the squirrels.

squirrel and dumplings
(drop biscuits)

Another dish I love is this one. Cut three squirrels in pieces and boil for 1½ to 3 hours until just before the meat begins to fall off the bones. Remove pieces from the pot and set broth aside for later use. Roll the pieces in seasoned flour, and brown them in a little oil in a big cast-iron skillet (make sure it is deep and has a good-fitting lid). Remove the squirrels and set aside. Then get busy making lots of gravy.

To make gravy, add hot broth to the skillet containing the drippings. Stir well. In a cup, mix some of the broth with flour to make a paste. Add that to the pan and whisk until gravy is thickened to your satisfaction. At this point, I usually add sautéed mushrooms and fresh garlic, parsley and black pepper. Add squirrel pieces to the gravy.

Make the drop biscuits using your favorite recipe. Drop the batter by heaping tablespoons atop the meat and gravy in the skillet. Place lid on tightly and cook on top of the stove until the dumplings are done.

A robust stew with a history as colorful as its ingredients, burgoo traditionally was made in the rural South with whatever meats and vegetables were in good supply. As I researched the recipe—which I had known of only by name before I made it for this book—I was struck by the various interpretations of the dish, the many origins of its name *and* its continued popularity. For example, burgoo fans from throughout the country (including those from annual festivals in Kentucky and Illinois) share thousands of their contemporary and century-old photos online. Many of the images feature crowds gathered 'round big iron burgoo kettles over wood fires. Folklorists blog about it, filmmakers have documented it, and even a Kentucky Derby winner was named after it. In any case, it's guaranteed to warm you on a cold day, and is pleasing to look at while it cooks—a confetti of colors in the pot.

Boone County burgoo with squirrel

Serves 6 to 8

2 pounds squirrel meat (about 4 squirrels)

2 tablespoons vegetable oil

6 cups water

1 cup white hominy

1½ cups lima beans (or other dried beans)

1 cup diced potatoes

2 carrots, diced

2 stalks celery, chopped

1 cup chopped onion

1 bay leaf

1 cup sliced okra (or fresh green beans)

1 to 2 red bell peppers, diced (or combination of sweet and hot roasted peppers)

1 28-ounce can diced tomatoes

1 cup fresh corn kernels

1½ to 2 teaspoons salt

½ teaspoon (or more) coarsely ground black pepper

½ to 1 teaspoon chile powder (depending upon desired heat)

½ teaspoon red-pepper sauce, such as Tabasco

1 teaspoon Worcestershire sauce

Clean 3 or 4 squirrels to obtain 2 pounds of meat on the bone. Rub the meat with salt and pepper and broil the whole squirrels for about 30 minutes (keeping squirrels about 8 inches from the heating element). Turn halfway through to brown both sides. Alternatively, you may put your squirrels in a large pot, cover them with water, and boil them for 2 to 3 hours (older squirrels take longer to cook until tender). Debone and cut into bite-sized pieces.

Heat oil in the bottom of a big pot and brown squirrel pieces for 4 or 5 minutes, turning them frequently. Add water to the pot and then the hominy, lima beans, potatoes, carrots, celery, onion and bay leaf. Simmer for 1 hour and skim off grease (if any).

Add okra, bell pepper, tomatoes, corn, salt, pepper, chile powder, Tabasco and Worcestershire sauces. Bring the stew back to a boil, stir well, and reduce heat. Simmer, partially covered for 2 more hours or until it is as thick as you like.

more burgoo bits

I took great liberty with the base recipe I used for this dish—substituting yellow onions for wild leeks, green beans for okra, speckled butter beans for white ones, fire-roasted hot and sweet peppers for bell peppers, and canned tomatoes for fresh. I also cooked it until it was a thick soup, not the "rib-sticking mass" suggested. I did, however, follow the exact order to serve it with johnnycakes, whiskey and water—a fine idea, probably derived from the tradition of burgoo making at barbecues and hunting camps.

My recipe is an adaptation of one I found in *Renewing America's Food Traditions, Saving and Savoring the Continent's Most Endangered Foods.* This fascinating book is a call to recognize, celebrate and conserve the vast diversity of foods that gives North America its culinary identity and reflects our multicultural heritage. It reminds us that "what we choose to eat can either conserve or deplete the cornucopia of our continent."

Game birds

game birds
delicious choices on the wing

Whether their quarry is the state's largest game birds (wild turkeys) or smallest (mourning doves), Missouri bird hunters are passionate about their sport. In the dogwood-laced forests of April, the harvested cornfields of October or the sleet-pelted wetlands of December, they'll spend thousands of hours each year. When they bring home their bounty, you also can be sure they will spend a fair amount of time cooking up some wonderful dishes to showcase their efforts.

John Schneller, a waterfowler and fine-food enthusiast from Boone County, talks about how his love of duck hunting evolved.

"My interest in duck hunting dates to childhood outings on the salt marshes adjacent to the Delaware Bay. Once I discovered there were marshes in Missouri, the gravitational pull took me to Ted Shanks, Fountain Grove and other long-standing public wetlands." John says he didn't have much in the way of duck-hunting skills until Mac Johnson (retired *Missouri Conservationist* editor) entered the picture.

"I remember when Mac invited me to a cornfield near Malta Bend for the dedication of a new wetland named Grand Pass. As any serious waterfowler in these parts knows, Grand Pass has evolved into one of the most sought-after duck-hunting marshes in the nation. Mac taught me how to call ducks, set out decoys and other nuances that were important for successful hunts.

"Our times together in the marsh made for memories we could never have imagined: a bald eagle dropping a drake mallard from its talons into our decoy spread or canoeing into a flock of 20,000 snow geese in dense fog before daybreak.

"In the spirit of Mac, I've tried my best to pass along the tradition to another generation. My daughter, Katherine, has been going out in the duck marsh since she was little—and she's developed quite a taste for ducks. Before she left for college she killed her first duck at Grand Pass—not far from the site of the dedication."

John says that a hunting buddy's version of rumaki is one of his favorite ways to eat duck. His friend's recipe wasn't available, but another one is. See page 60 for *George Seek's Duck Rumaki.*

Peak numbers of mallards arrive at Missouri's wetlands in late-November or early-December. These ducks end up on more tables than any other species of waterfowl.

This is a rustic, cold-weather dish inspired by the classic southwestern French casserole, of which there are innumerable versions. Most are based upon a stew of white beans and various kinds of pork and fowl. This recipe—simpler than many—is a combination of techniques and ingredients from two versions I admire. The dish gets its name from the earthenware in which it is traditionally baked—the cassole.

Columbia cassoulet
with smoked pork and duck

Serves 6

Beans

1 pound dried small navy beans

1½ teaspoons salt

8 cups cold water

2 cups chicken broth

1 tablespoon tomato paste (See note below.)

2 cups chopped onions

2 tablespoons finely chopped garlic

Bouquet garni

3 fresh or dried thyme sprigs

1 bay leaf

1 3-inch piece celery, cut into thirds

3 whole cloves

3 fresh flat-leaf parsley sprigs, plus 4 tablespoons chopped leaves (to be used later)

¼ teaspoon whole black peppercorns

Meat

3 tablespoons extra-virgin olive oil

1 pound Polish sausage (or combination of smoked sausage and cooked smoked ham hock), cut into bite-sized chunks

2 carrots, coarsely chopped

1 14-ounce can diced tomatoes

4 or 5 smoked (or roasted) duck breasts, cut into 1-inch chunks (See *Easy Tea-Smoked Duck* on page 58.)

Salt and freshly ground pepper

Bread-crumb topping

2 cups fresh coarse bread crumbs (from good, rustic white bread)

2 tablespoons extra-virgin olive oil

2 tablespoons reserved chopped parsley

½ teaspoon salt

¼ teaspoon freshly ground pepper

Equipment: 8-inch square of cheesecloth

In a large pot, cover beans with cold water and soak 8 to 12 hours; or boil 2 minutes and let soak 1 hour. Drain beans and put back in pot. Add salt, water, broth, tomato paste, onions and garlic. Put thyme, bay leaf, celery, cloves, parsley sprigs and peppercorns in an 8-inch square of cheesecloth and tie into a bundle with food-safe white string to make a bouquet garni. Add bouquet garni to pot, and stir to distribute flavors. Bring to a boil, then reduce heat and simmer, uncovered, until beans are almost tender, about 1 hour.

Heat olive oil in skillet. Add sausage and carrots and brown lightly for 5 to 8 minutes. Add tomatoes with their juice and cook on medium-high 5 minutes. Add contents of skillet to beans, cover and simmer 1 hour. Skim off excess fat and discard bouquet garni.

Add duck and 2 tablespoons reserved chopped parsley to pot, stir well and ladle into a 4- to 5-quart cast-iron or earthenware pot, distributing meat and beans evenly. The meat and beans should be level with the liquid. If they are submerged, ladle excess liquid back into pot and boil until reduced; then pour it back into casserole dish—this gives the liquid a nice concentrated flavor. Mix bread-crumb ingredients well, and spread evenly atop casserole. Bake, uncovered, in lower third of 375°F oven for about 1 hour. Top should be golden.

Serve with a mixed green salad and a chewy, coarse-textured bread for sopping up the juices. A Pinot Noir would accompany nicely.

This is a wonderfully versatile main-course salad with a delightful combination of ingredients that can be increased, omitted or substituted depending upon your taste. For instance, leave out the pomegranate seeds if you absolutely can't get your hands on one, and add dried cranberries or cherries or fresh blueberries or raspberries. Don't have an apple? Add a pear instead. Don't like arugula? Use spinach. You even may substitute turkey for duck.

smoked duck salad

Serves 2 to 4

Dressing

4 tablespoons fresh orange juice

¼ cup extra-virgin olive oil

2 teaspoons fresh lemon juice

2 teaspoons fresh pomegranate juice, squeezed from a few unused seeds (optional)

½ teaspoon Dijon mustard

Pinch of paprika

Pinch of sugar

Salt

Coarsely ground black pepper

Salad

2 smoked duck breasts, cut into thin strips (See *Easy Tea-Smoked Duck* below.)

3 tangerines or 2 small oranges (save 4 tablespoons of juice for dressing)

1 small apple

1 small red onion

8 cups mixed lettuces (any combination you prefer; I like radicchio, Belgian endive, Romaine, Boston and a bit of arugula)

⅓ cup pecan halves, toasted

4 tablespoons fresh pomegranate seeds

Whisk first seven ingredients (through sugar) together in a small bowl until well blended. Season to taste with salt and pepper. Add smoked duck strips to bowl and let marinate (at least 15 minutes) while preparing the rest of the salad.

Separate tangerines into segments. If using oranges, cut off peels and white pith; cut each segment in half. Cut apple into matchstick-sized pieces or thin slices. Slice onion into thin rings. Set all aside. Strain dressing from the duck and reserve. Toss lettuces in a large bowl with enough of the reserved dressing to coat lightly, but well.

Divide lettuces among 4 salad plates. Top each with duck strips, oranges, apple and onion rings. Sprinkle with pecans and pomegranate seeds. Drizzle with remaining dressing if desired.

If you want smoked duck, but don't have time to prepare a traditional smoker, try this quick-cooking method. I was skeptical when I ran across this idea, but it works.

easy tea-smoked duck

2 duck breasts

2 ounces brown sugar

2 ounces black tea leaves (such as Darjeeling)

2 ounces uncooked white rice

Place a piece of foil in the bottom of a medium sauté pan. In a small bowl, combine the sugar, tea and rice. Pour the entire mixture onto the foil, and cover with another piece of foil. Place the duck breasts on the foil, and cover the pan with a lid. Cook over medium heat for 20 minutes or until the duck is cooked through but still slightly pink. Remove from pan and slice on the diagonal into strips.

ducks are what they eat

Ducks that eat a lot of grains during the winter months—mallards, teal, gadwalls, wigeons and pintails—generally have a milder flavor than diving ducks and shovelers, which eat mainly fish and invertebrates. However, proper rinsing, marinating and cooking will convert even the "fishiest" duck into a delectable meal.

Here's a tasty, bite-sized treat that shows up on quite a few Missouri duck hunters' party tables. Legend has it that it's based upon the "Polynesian" appetizer made famous by Trader Vic's restaurant chain. This version was passed on to me by Matt Seek, an editor for the Conservation Department. He inherited it from his avid waterfowl-hunting father, George Seek, the agency's former Private Lands Division chief. George avers that the success of this dish depends upon the treatment of the birds, so be sure to follow his tips. The crunchy-smoky-meaty morsels are delicious, and should make those of a certain age nostalgic for the charm of the Trader's rattan-and-tiki-torch ambience and outlandish beverages.

George Seek's duck rumaki

Serves a crowd (if you have enough time and duck)

Duck breast meat, cut into ¼-inch strips
Soy sauce
Teriyaki sauce, purchased or homemade
One can sliced water chestnuts
Locally produced, good-quality smoked
   bacon, each strip cut in half
Sharp, round toothpicks

Once all the blood is removed from the duck strips (see George's tips before you begin), soak them overnight in a one-to-one combination of soy and teriyaki sauces. Remove strips from the sauce—and using one water-chestnut slice per duck strip—wrap a strip of duck around the chestnut. Secure with a toothpick. Next, wrap a half strip of bacon around the entire duck/water chestnut and secure to the ends of the toothpick. Place back in soy/teriyaki marinade.

Start you charcoal (George says only unrefined city folks use a gas grill) and drink a beer or two (maybe three, depending upon whether you used good-quality charcoal) until the coals are nearly all white. When the coals are ready, place the rumaki on the grill and watch very closely—flaming bacon grease is hard to put out! Keep the lid on your grill to prevent flaming, and leave it open only for the last minute or two to brown. The rumaki should be ready in 10 to 15 minutes (when the bacon is fully cooked). Do not overcook!

Pull from fire and immediately eat. The proper way to eat rumaki is to hold the toothpick between your thumb and forefinger, place the entire bite in your mouth and withdraw the toothpick. Amberbach is the preferred beer for rumaki; a Syrah also stands up nicely and complements the bold flavors of this appetizer.

George's tips
- Try not to breast-shoot your ducks.
- To clean your birds, use your thumbs to pull back the skin from the breast and a sharp knife to fillet the meat away from the breast bone.
- Cut breasts against the grain into ¼-inch strips.
- For a real treat, save back all the duck tenderloins (the small strip of meat tucked up against the backbone). Set aside for the cooks or that special person you're trying to impress. As with most tenderloins, these pieces are sweet and tender by nature. Marinate and cook in the same way as the breast strips.
- Soak in saltwater, rinsing and changing water frequently to ensure the removal of blood from the meat. The "liver" taste in ducks is caused by the blood, not the meat.

Avid duck hunter Jim Low offers a Missouri twist on the Indonesian national dish, which often features chicken. These are good as appetizers or as a light meal accompanied by hot rice and a salad.

Jim Low's sassafras-marinated mallard satay
with Thai peanut dipping sauce

Serves 4 to 6 as an appetizer

4 mallard breasts
½ cup soy sauce
½ cup red wine
4 garlic cloves, crushed
2 tablespoons grated fresh ginger root (peeled)
Juice of 1 fresh lime

Equipment: A dozen 6- by 1-inch sticks of sassafras (or hickory)
6 long bamboo skewers soaked in water

Cut breasts into ¾-inch strips. Combine remainder of ingredients (except sassafras) in a bowl and add the duck. Marinate at least 1 hour or overnight.

Soak sassafras wood in water overnight. The next day, drain the wood and spread the sticks over a generous amount of charcoal briquettes on one side of a kettle-type grill.

Thread breast strips evenly onto six bamboo skewers (see *Soak Your Skewers* on page 22) and place them on the opposite side of the grill so they will cook over indirect heat. Cook until just pink in the middle; take care not to overcook. Serve hot with *Thai Peanut Dipping Sauce*.

Thai peanut dipping sauce

2 teaspoons vegetable oil
4 garlic cloves, chopped
1 small fresh chile pepper, chopped
½ cup water
¼ cup soy sauce
⅓ cup 100 percent peanut butter, preferably crunchy
1 teaspoon brown sugar
Juice of 1 fresh lime

Heat oil in a small saucepan, and add garlic and pepper. Cook 5 to 10 seconds, taking care not to brown garlic.

Add remaining ingredients and cook until thickened—3 or 4 minutes. Serve sauce warm or at room temperature.

This is a version of a tagine, a classic Moroccan stew. It can be made with many different meats including quail, beef, lamb and chicken. Pigeon was featured in the one I had in Morocco many years ago. I think the combination of pungent spices and tomatoes complement the robust flavor of duck. Don't be put off by the long list of ingredients. It goes together very quickly, and while one thing is cooking, you easily can grind spices and prepare other parts. I spent 1½ hours from the beginning of prep to the finished dish. By the way, the $650 recipe subtitle reflects how much it cost to repair my tooth after I broke it on the steel shot found in one of the ducks. So, just a precautionary note: Check for shot carefully before you begin cooking!

mallard stew with tomato and eggplant (the $650 duck dinner)

Serves 4 to 6

6 tablespoons extra-virgin olive oil

3 cups sliced onions

5 to 6 large garlic cloves, minced

1 tablespoon paprika

1½ teaspoons salt

1 teaspoon turmeric

1 teaspoon ground coriander

1 teaspoon ground fennel seeds

1 teaspoon coarsely ground black pepper

½ teaspoon ground cumin

½ teaspoon ground ginger

1 28-ounce can diced tomatoes

1 cup water

Juice of 1 medium lemon

8 mallard breasts

1 large eggplant, unpeeled and
   cut into 1-inch cubes

½ teaspoon dried marjoram or
   1 tablespoon chopped fresh

½ cup whole or slivered almonds, toasted

Handful fresh cilantro, chopped

Rice or couscous

Heat 2 tablespoons olive oil in large, wide pot over medium heat. Add onions and garlic. Cover and cook until onions are soft, about 10 minutes, stirring several times.

Add next eight ingredients (through ginger); stir for 1 minute. Stir in tomatoes, water and lemon juice. Bring to a slow boil. Arrange breasts in a single layer in pot, and spoon some sauce over them. Reduce heat to medium-low, cover and simmer 15 minutes. Turn duck over, cover and simmer until duck is tender, about 15 minutes longer. Remove duck to a plate and cover.

Meanwhile, preheat oven to 400°F. Rub large, rimmed baking sheet with olive oil. Place eggplant and remaining 4 tablespoons olive oil in a large bowl and toss to coat. Spread eggplant on baking sheet and bake 20 minutes or until soft and brown, stirring two or three times.

Stir eggplant and marjoram into pot. Simmer uncovered 10 minutes. Season stew to taste with more lemon juice if desired, and salt and pepper. Add duck to reheat briefly in sauce.

The duck may be presented on a bed of rice or couscous on a large platter, with sauce atop. However, my preference is to remove breasts from the pot, slice each into 8 or 10 pieces and plate two breasts per serving, topped with sauce. Serve atop rice or place rice alongside duck. Sprinkle with almonds and cilantro.

Accompany with a salad of spinach, arugula and Romaine dressed with a Dijon vinaigrette and topped with sliced fresh pears and blue cheese. A sturdy wine such as Cabernet, Shiraz or Merlot goes well.

I love to make fried rice whenever I have a nice bit of leftover meat and a few colorful vegetables in the fridge. I often use chicken or pork, but have found that wild turkey works beautifully, as well. Use your imagination when it comes to vegetables. Mushrooms are good additions, as are broccoli and snow peas.

wild-turkey fried rice

Serves 4

Seasoning the turkey

1½ cups cooked wild turkey, diced

1½ teaspoons soy sauce

1 teaspoon vegetable oil

Pinch of salt and freshly ground black pepper

Assembling the dish

I tablespoon vegetable oil

3 eggs, slightly beaten and seasoned with salt and freshly ground black pepper

2 strips thick bacon, cut into ½-inch pieces

3 green onions, whites chopped and greens reserved

1 large slice (about ¼-inch thick) peeled fresh ginger root, minced

1 large garlic clove, minced

1½ cups fresh mung-bean sprouts

1 carrot, slices cut diagonally and then in thirds

1 medium sweet red pepper, sliced and cut diagonally

4 tablespoons peanut (or vegetable) oil

1 teaspoon salt

5 cups cold rice (See *Cold Rice for Good Results.*)

1 tablespoon (or more) soy sauce

Freshly ground black pepper

Place diced turkey in a small bowl and season the turkey with soy, oil, salt and pepper. Cover and refrigerate while preparing the eggs and vegetables.

Assemble all ingredients within easy reach of wok.

Set wok over medium-high heat. Add vegetable oil; when the oil is hot and shimmering, add eggs and scramble until well done. Remove and set aside.

Clean wok with paper towel and heat again. Add bacon, stirring often until browned, but not crisp. Remove, drain on paper towels and set aside. Drain all but a tablespoon of grease from the wok.

Add green onion whites, ginger and garlic, stirring quickly and constantly. Add turkey and stir again. Add bean sprouts, carrot and red pepper. Cook about 2 minutes, being careful not to overcook. Vegetables should be cooked, but still firm and a little crunchy. Remove all from wok into a bowl.

Return wok to heat and add peanut oil until hot. Add salt and then rice. Stir fry about 3 minutes to heat and coat rice evenly. Add soy sauce and black pepper and stir. Add eggs, meats and vegetables, and stir well to combine.

Turn onto platter and top with green onion greens. Serve with *Spicy Cucumber Salad.*

cold rice for good results

Rice must be cold for this dish to be successful. I often cook it a day in advance and refrigerate. Freshly cooked rice, if used, will turn to mush when fried.

The long, narrow, almost-seedless variety works best for this dish. I use an Asian cucumber, which grows in great abundance in my garden. Its skin is sweet and doesn't need to be peeled. These and other similar varieties also are common at farmers markets and in some grocery stores.

spicy cucumber salad   Serves 4

2 medium Asian cucumbers
¼ cup rice vinegar
2 teaspoons soy sauce
1 teaspoon sesame oil
½ teaspoon salt
1 tablespoon sesame seeds
1 teaspoon sugar, if desired
Sprinkle of freshly minced hot pepper (or dried hot pepper flakes) to taste

Cut cucumbers lengthwise, scoop out seeds and slice crosswise into ¼-inch-thick pieces. In a glass or ceramic bowl, combine the remaining ingredients and mix well. Add cucumbers and toss to coat thoroughly. Chill slightly before serving.

Here's a delicious way to use up those leftover turkey scraps from a roasted or grilled bird. Bathe them in this easy and delicious corn soup. Make it when corn is at its peak sweetness in Missouri.

wild turkey and summer sweet-corn soup

Makes 6 cups of soup

Soup

3 ears of fresh sweet corn
3 cups whole milk
2 tablespoons butter
1 large onion, chopped
1 large carrot, thinly sliced
1 celery stalk, thinly sliced
1 large garlic clove, minced
2 cups water
2 large fresh thyme sprigs
2 fresh rosemary sprigs
1 bay leaf
6 ounces cooked turkey (1 to 1½ cups)
Freshly ground white pepper
Two pinches of Spanish smoked paprika

Garnish

1 small sweet red pepper, diced
2 green onions, thinly sliced
2 tablespoons chopped fresh chives

Cut kernels from cobs and reserve. Break cobs in half. Bring milk and corncob halves (not kernels) just to boil in medium pot. Remove from heat, cover and let steep while sautéing vegetables.

Melt butter in large saucepan over medium heat. Add onion and a pinch of salt, and sauté until translucent, about 5 minutes. Add corn kernels, carrot, celery and garlic; cook until vegetables are soft, stirring frequently, about 15 minutes. Add water, thyme and rosemary sprigs, bay leaf, and milk with corncobs. Increase heat and bring to boil. Cover partially, reduce heat to low, and simmer 20 minutes.

Discard corncobs, herb sprigs and bay leaf. Cool soup slightly. Purée half of soup in blender until smooth (taking care to press firmly on the lid with your hand during processing to prevent hot liquid from flying out of the top of the blender).

Pour contents of blender back into saucepan with remaining soup. Add turkey and stir. Reheat briefly. Season to taste with salt, white pepper and paprika. Divide among bowls. Garnish with red pepper, green onions and chives.

W hip up a batch of this New Orleans-inspired relish to make delicious sandwiches with turkey leftovers.

wild-turkey muffuletta sandwiches

Relish

¾ cup chopped red onion

½ cup chopped sweet red pepper

1 stalk celery, chopped

½ cup calamata olives, pitted

½ cup drained small Spanish
   pimiento-stuffed green olives

¼ cup extra-virgin olive oil

2 tablespoons drained capers

2 tablespoons chopped parsley

12 fresh basil leaves, roughly sliced

1 teaspoon chopped fresh oregano

1 teaspoon chopped fresh chives

1 tablespoon red wine vinegar

Freshly ground black pepper

Sandwich

1 24-inch-long French or sourdough baguette,
   split lengthwise

12 ounces cooked wild turkey breast, sliced

4 ounces Jarlsberg or good Swiss cheese, sliced

Tomato slices (optional)

Combine relish ingredients in food processor and chop finely. Add pepper to taste. Transfer to bowl. Let stand 1 hour at room temperature.

Spread half of muffuletta relish over each cut side of bread. Place turkey and cheese on bottom half of bread. Top with tomato slices. Cover with top half of bread. Cut diagonally into 4 sandwiches.

"New Orleans food is as delicious as the less criminal forms of sin."

—Mark Twain

the Italian-American sandwich

Invented in the early 1900s by New Orleanians of Sicilian descent, the muffuletta is still a city favorite. Named after the thick, round loaf on which it customarily is made, the sandwich oozes with layers of cheese, various meats and olive salad.

This is my all-time favorite comfort-food supper for a cold winter's evening. A co-worker many years ago brought this to a potluck, and I was wise enough to wrestle away her family recipe. She used chicken, which is delicious, as well. This gem of a dish is elegant in its simplicity. The rich biscuit dough tops the tasty turkey, which is cloaked in a simple white sauce. I would imagine that other wild game such as dove, rabbit or squirrel could be substituted with equally fine results. Just remember to save the broth in which the meat is cooked.

wild-turkey dropped-biscuit pie

Serves 4

3 to 4 pounds of wild turkey meat on the bone

Sauce
3 tablespoons butter
3 tablespoons flour
1 cup cream

Dough
2 cups flour
1 teaspoon salt
2 teaspoons baking powder
2 tablespoons butter
1 egg, beaten
1 cup milk
Coarsely ground black pepper

Cover turkey in water and bring to a boil. Turn down the heat and simmer until tender. Remove meat from broth, cool and cut into 1-inch chunks or shred if preferred. Reserve broth.

Grease a Dutch oven or other casserole dish with a light coating of butter. Add turkey to the dish.

Make sauce

In a medium saucepan melt butter, whisk in flour and stir until well combined. Add 3 cups turkey broth and cream. Whisk, salt to taste and cook until it is a smooth sauce. It will be quite thin, but will thicken when baked with turkey. Pour sauce over turkey.

Make biscuit dough

Preheat oven to 350°F. Combine flour, salt and baking powder in a medium bowl and stir well. Rub 2 tablespoons butter into flour mixture until combined. Add egg and milk; mix well. Drop batter by heaping tablespoonfuls (12 to 16) over entire surface area of turkey/sauce. Bake for approximately 1 hour or more until biscuits are nicely browned. Sauce will appear thin when you remove the dish from the oven. However, it will thicken nicely if you allow the dish to cool for a few minutes before spooning it into shallow bowls. Grind a few twists of fresh black pepper atop and serve.

Accompany with lightly steamed broccoli or a salad of mixed, fresh greens. An unoaked Chardonnay accompanies nicely.

use the whole bird

Although the breast is the prime choice on a turkey, the remaining meat can be used as a base for a flavorful soup or for any other number of dishes, including this one. Considering the patience and skill required to bag this bird, it's a shame to use the breast and throw out the rest.

Craig Cyr, chef/owner of The Wine Cellar & Bistro in Columbia, created this magnificent treatment for quail. Featured on his menu as an appetizer, this dish also would make a wonderful main course if you allowed about two quail per serving. The rich, savory spoon pudding is a must to accompany the exotically spiced birds.

Craig Cyr's Moroccan spice-rubbed quail with sweet-onion pistachio spoon pudding

Serves 4 to 6

10 whole quail, butterflied (To butterfly, cut each quail along both sides of its backbone. Remove the bone and spread the bird flat.)

Spice rub

2 teaspoons ground cinnamon
2 teaspoons cumin seeds, toasted
1 teaspoon coriander seeds, toasted
¼ cup paprika
¼ teaspoon ground cloves
1 teaspoon ground ginger
Coarsely ground black pepper, 3 or 4 cranks of the pepper mill
Salt, to taste

Cilantro-garlic marinade

1 bunch fresh cilantro, finely chopped
3 garlic cloves, minced
½ cup extra-virgin olive oil

Grind all spices together with a mortar and pestle, or with a coffee or spice grinder. Set aside.

In a small bowl, mix cilantro and garlic with olive oil. Rub quail with marinade mixture and then coat with spice rub. Marinate for an hour or so. Grill over medium heat, moving to indirect heat after grill marks are achieved. Baste quail with remaining marinade during process. Cook to internal temperature of 165°F. Serve with the spoon pudding.

sweet-onion pistachio spoon pudding

½ medium onion, thinly sliced
1 carrot, shaved
1 tablespoon chopped garlic
1 tablespoon butter
1 cup toasted ground pistachios
½ teaspoon ground cumin
4 large eggs
2 cups cream
½ cup golden raisins
Salt and coarsely ground pepper

Preheat oven to 350°F. Sauté onion, carrot and garlic in butter until tender; add pistachios and cumin and sauté a minute longer.

In a separate bowl, mix the eggs and cream together; add onion, carrot and nut mixture. Then fold in the raisins and season to taste with salt and pepper. Pour in a buttered 9-inch glass (or ceramic) pie pan and bake until set all the way through.

Here's a rich and quick pasta dish created by avid hunter Kevin Lohraff, the Conservation Department's education programs supervisor. "I don't shoot as many quail as I'd like," says Kevin. "I think few hunters do. If you'd like to take your too-few quail and stretch them into a tasty dish for three to four people, I recommend this combination. Use as many 'stretching' ingredients as you wish."

Kevin Lohraff's quail-stretching pasta

Serves 4

1 pound bow-tie pasta
Quail, pheasants, rabbits or squirrels
Olive oil for sautéing

Stretchers
Fresh peas, broccoli, asparagus, mushrooms, sweet red pepper, onion

Sauce
1 stick butter
2 to 3 tablespoons flour
1 to 1½ cups half and half or cream
1 to 1½ cups grated Parmigiano-Reggiano or Romano cheese
2 to 3 garlic cloves, minced
Coarsely ground black pepper

Start boiling water for pasta. Cut quail or pheasant meat off the bone and chop into bite-sized pieces (chill the birds first to make this easier). Sauté meat in a little olive oil just until pink disappears in the middle. If you substitute rabbit or squirrel, you will need to boil them first for 1½ to 2½ hours before chopping. Set meat aside.

Lightly steam green vegetables or sauté other stretchers in a little olive oil until they are as done as you like them. Set aside.

Melt butter in a medium saucepan and whisk in flour until well combined. Add half and half and cheese, stirring to blend well. After cheese is melted, add garlic and black pepper.

Add meat and stretchers to the saucepan, and give a stir to combine well. Toss with pasta.

Good eatin'!

"Don't eat anything your great grandmother wouldn't recognize as food."

—Michael Pollan

penne with pheasant in morel cream sauce

1 cup pheasant meat (See *Stew the pheasant.*)

⅓ cup dried morel mushrooms

4 tablespoons butter

1½ tablespoons shallots, minced

1 cup heavy cream

1½ tablespoons finely chopped Italian parsley

½ pound penne or garganelli pasta

Dash of freshly grated nutmeg

Stew the pheasant

Place whole pheasant in pot with enough lightly salted water to cover the bird. Bring to a boil, then reduce heat to medium, cover and cook until tender. Remove bird and reserve broth. Pull meat from bones and cut into generous bite-sized pieces. Set aside.

Make the pasta and sauce

Soak morels in 1 cup hot water until plump, about 30 minutes. Remove mushrooms, reserving soaking water. Gently dry and chop mushrooms into bite-sized pieces. Set aside.

Melt butter in a large sauté pan. Add shallots and sauté until tender. Add cream, 1½ to 2 cups pheasant broth, and all of mushroom broth; gently boil to reduce sauce by almost half. Cook pasta in large pot of salted water while sauce reduces. When sauce is thickened and reduced to your liking, add parsley, pheasant and morels. Season with salt and pepper to taste.

Toss with freshly cooked pasta, taste again for seasoning, and sprinkle with freshly grated nutmeg. Serve at once, accompanied by a dry Riesling.

This is a wonderful brunch or light-dinner dish. The earthy mushrooms and spinach, as well as the liquid ingredients, provide just the right amount of moisture to plump up the pheasant meat, which tends to be a bit on the dry side. I had locally grown shiitake mushrooms on hand, but native Missouri mushrooms would be even better. I'm also guessing that wild turkey would be a fine stand-in for pheasant. The pudding keeps well for several days after baking; store tightly wrapped in the refrigerator.

savory pheasant bread pudding

Serves 4 to 6

4 cups bread cubes (½-inch size and preferably a combination of coarse-textured white and whole-wheat)

½ cup finely chopped onion

5 tablespoons unsalted butter

4 ounces shiitake mushrooms, cut into bite-sized ¼-inch-thick pieces

1 cup cooked pheasant meat, cut into bite-sized pieces

5 ounces fresh spinach, coarsely chopped

1 cup pheasant or chicken broth

2 tablespoons finely chopped flat-leaf parsley

2 large garlic cloves, minced

2 cups half and half

4 large eggs

½ cup grated Parmigiano-Reggiano cheese

½ teaspoon salt

¼ teaspoon coarsely ground pepper

Fresh nutmeg

Preheat oven to 350°F. Place the bread cubes in a single layer in a large, shallow baking pan and toast in oven until golden-brown (turning as needed) about 10 minutes. Set aside to cool.

Cook onion in butter in a large, heavy skillet over medium heat, stirring occasionally until pieces begin to soften, about 3 minutes. Add mushrooms, salt and coarsely ground pepper to taste; cook about 5 minutes. Add pheasant, spinach, broth, parsley and garlic; cook, stirring, about 5 minutes. At the end of cooking time, there should be just enough liquid in the skillet to moisten contents. Remove from heat.

In a large bowl, whisk together half and half, eggs, cheese, salt, pepper and a few gratings of nutmeg. Stir in skillet ingredients and bread cubes until well coated. Let stand 10 minutes for bread to soften. Bake in a buttered, 2-quart shallow baking dish for 30 to 35 minutes until puffed and lightly browned.

Accompany with a mixed green salad and a sturdy white wine such as Sicilian Grillo or an Austrian Gruner Veltliner.

Jim Low, longtime Conservation Department newsman and waterfowl hunter, made this gumbo one year at the agency's annual Beast Feast in Jefferson City. Every December, usually in the week preceding Christmas, employees from each of the agency's divisions provide lunch for the entire central office staff. They cook up their best native Missouri game, fish, mushroom, nut and fruit recipes and try to outdo one another in the process. This hearty stew, which won the "Best Recipe" title at the 2009 feast, was one of my favorites. Jim didn't measure ingredient quantities when concocting this large amount, but he made an educated guess for this cookbook. Here's the basic idea to follow when you have a hungry crowd to feed and want to free up some space in your freezer.

Jim Low's Beast Feast gumbo

Serves a throng

2 cups extra-virgin olive oil

3 cups flour

4 cups chopped yellow onions

4 cups chopped celery

2 cups chopped bell peppers

½ cup finely chopped garlic

1 pound tasso, thinly sliced

1 pound andouille, sliced into ¼-inch-thick chunks

2 to 4 pounds of meat (waterfowl, upland game birds and venison cut into bite-sized pieces)

1 pound of fish, broiled and boned

6 quarts stock (chicken, goose or pheasant)

2 teaspoons ground cayenne pepper

6 to 12 small dried hot peppers, whole

24 ounces crushed canned tomatoes

6 chicken livers

2 small packages of frozen okra, or equivalent of fresh

4 cups sliced green onions

2 cups chopped parsley

Salt and coarsely ground pepper

Cooked rice

Filé powder

Place oil in large (about 15-quart), cast-iron Dutch oven over medium-high heat until hot. Add flour a little at a time, whisking constantly until the mixture turns golden brown. Start over if black spots appear.

Add yellow onions, celery, bell peppers and garlic, and sauté, stirring constantly, until vegetables start to soften. Add tasso, andouille, game and fish; mix well and sauté another 10 to 15 minutes to develop flavor. Add stock a little at a time, whisking constantly to prevent lumps. Transfer to an electric roaster such as one you would use to bake a turkey. Add cayenne, hot peppers, tomatoes and chicken livers. Give a big stir, cover and cook at 250°F for at least 2 hours. If time allows, cooking overnight is better.

Add okra, green onions and parsley 15 minutes before serving. Season to taste with salt and pepper. Ladle over cooked rice and sprinkle with filé powder.

"A recipe is only a theme, which an intelligent cook can play each time with a variation."

—Madame Benoît

a merry mix of meat and fish

In the version I tried there were ample pieces of duck, coot, goose, dove, pheasant, venison, crappie, catfish and bass. Obviously, you may vary the mix to suit your taste or hunting and fishing success.

"Gumbo is a great place to use game that is less-than-prime table fare," says Jim. "Coots, shovelers, mergansers and other diving ducks are right at home in this dish. Opossum, raccoon, beaver and other specialty meats are unlikely to be recognized and very much in keeping with Cajuns' catholic taste in game."

ingredient tips

Tasso (Cajun dried pork seasoned with cayenne, garlic and salt, then heavily smoked) provides most of the seasoning in this gumbo, says Jim. Consequently, substitute at your own risk!

Andouille (a popular spicy Cajun smoked pork sausage) is less critical to the mix, but preferred. Kielbasa can be substituted.

Look for both pork products in stores that have a good selection of ethnic cured meats. Online sources also are available. If you live in Boone County, then you might take advantage of the opportunity to purchase locally made tasso and andouille. Students in the Culinary Arts program at Columbia Area Career Center cure meats and offer them for sale several times a year. The meats are produced under the guidance of instructor Brook Harlan, whose culinary career includes impressive experience with Cajun cured meats.

Filé powder is the powdered leaves of the sassafras tree. Long before the use of filé powder for Creole and Cajun cooking, the Choctaw people pounded sassafras leaves into a powder and added them to soups and stews.

Many tasty meals await the tables of several Missouri waterfowl hunters.

Fish

fish
a world of good eatin' in the state's waters

I'll never forget sneaking my first bite of creamy white, golden-crusted catfish from between the paper towels when I was 6 or 7 years old. My mother had just scooped it out of the frying pan before supper, but I couldn't wait until it got to the table. My uncle, an avid Cuivre River fisherman, kept our family's freezer stocked with catfish and carp. Consequently, I had many opportunities to repeat my stealthy behavior whenever the irresistible sizzling sounds and smells of frying fish wafted from the kitchen during my childhood. Since then I've enjoyed cooking and eating many more kinds of Missouri sport fish, but catfish with cornbread holds a special place in my heart.

With almost a million fishing permits sold in the state annually, it's obvious that fish rank high in the hearts and kitchens of many Missourians. Although there are more than 200 species of fish in the Show-Me State, anglers focus on only about two dozen of them. Bass, crappie, catfish and trout—in that order—are the most popular. Although not a native species, trout stocked in the state's cold streams have drawn fly fishers from near and far. In fact, Missouri has become one of the top five trout-fishing spots in the nation.

Trout draw many anglers not only for their outstanding culinary possibilities, but also for the "auditory and visual vacation" fishing for trout provides. That's how angler Theresa Ferrugia, who took up the sport eight years ago, describes her time in the water. "I love the sounds of the running water, the birds and the wind … and seeing the eagles, osprey, kingfishers, hummingbirds and flowers along the banks, rocks and boulders. Of course, the colors of the fish themselves are gorgeous.

"Even though my husband and I go fishing together, most of the time we don't even fish within sight of each other. I really enjoy fishing by myself—the time passes so quickly. Boat fishing is not for me, because I love to wade. In the winter I use waders and boots, but in the summer I wet wade, using only boots. My passion is dry fly fishing, and the most challenging thing about it is what combination of colors to use, how to present the fly, and how the trout might be taking the fly on a particular day.

"I have seen the most amazing things while fishing—an eagle and an osprey fighting in midair over a fish; a guy running upstream because he just saw a bear cross the river; and three or four eagles soaring against the bluffs. It's all wonderful!"

Theresa enjoys casting her line on the Current River, between Montauk State Park and Baptist Camp.

MARK GUTCHEN

Flathead catfish

Anglers Kevin Lohraff and his son, Finn, show off their paddlefish, taken from the Mississippi River near Hannibal. Paddlefish (also known as spoonbill) are prehistoric fish found only in the tributaries of the Mississippi and Missouri rivers and in the Yangtze River in China. Since they are filter feeders, they will not accept bait or lures and must be caught by snagging. They are threatened by poachers, who take the fish illegally to sell their eggs for caviar.

The Conservation Department raises young paddlefish at Blind Pony Hatchery in Sweet Springs to stock the waters of Table Rock and Truman lakes, and Lake of the Ozarks. Although short on good looks, the fish makes for some fine eatin' and even a beautiful-looking dish. See *Smoked Paddlefish Niçoise* on page 114.

A dish strongly associated with the west coast of Mexico, seviche traditionally is made with raw fish (scallops, shrimp or other saltwater fish). The fish is "cooked" by marinating it in fresh lime juice. Cooking fish this way also is common on the other side of the Pacific (in Southeast Asia) and in Central and South America. If eating fish raw makes you squeamish—relax. In this Americanized version, the fish is cooked with heat. This makes a beautiful and refreshing summer appetizer, especially when presented in martini glasses.

freshwater seviche

Serves 4 generously as an appetizer or 2 as a main dish

3 medium limes

1 pound bass, bluegill or crappie fillets (or a combination of all)

1 small red onion, diced

1 small sweet red pepper, diced

1 cup diced cucumber

1 to 2 jalapenos, finely chopped

1 tablespoon extra-virgin olive oil

1 teaspoon finely chopped fresh thyme

½ teaspoon (or more to taste) finely chopped fresh oregano, dill or basil—or a combination of all

1 avocado, diced

12 cherry tomatoes, halved (any kind or color)

3 tablespoons finely chopped cilantro, plus several sprigs for garnish

½ teaspoon salt

Squeeze the juice from one of the limes into a medium saucepan. Then add the two squeezed rinds and 1 quart of water. Cover and simmer over medium-low heat for 10 minutes.

Raise the heat to high, add the fillets, cover and let the liquid return to a full boil. Immediately remove from the heat, hold the lid askew and drain off all liquid. Set the pan of fish aside, tightly covered for 2 minutes (depending on thickness of fillets) to finish cooking. Spread fish out on a cookie sheet to cool.

Break fish into bite-sized pieces into a medium bowl. Add juice from remaining 2 limes (about ⅓ cup), onion, red pepper, cucumber, jalapenos, olive oil, herbs, avocado, tomatoes, cilantro and salt. Cover and let stand at room temperature ½ hour.

Serve in martini glasses, garnished with cilantro sprigs and whole lime slices. Accompany with a small bowl of tortilla chips. This also makes a light and tasty summer meal for two people. Serve on a bed of fresh greens and eat with warm, whole-wheat tortillas.

heirloom cherry tomatoes

While any cherry tomato will work, I love to use several different heirloom varieties when they are abundant in my garden or at the farmers market. Tiny super-sweet yellow ones lend a delicate flavor, and those beautiful black cherries are equally luscious in this dish.

This hearty fish stew has as many colorful stories attributed to its origin as there are ways to make it. Most agree that the dish was born on San Francisco's waterfront before World War II among Italian and Portuguese immigrant fishermen. No matter the history, cioppino is a delicious party dish and a great way to use odds and ends from a variety of fish. Use the following as a guide, but feel free to toss in whatever Missouri fish you have on hand and whatever is freshest. Crayfish would be a good addition to the pot, as well.

cioppino

Serves 4 to 6

4 large garlic cloves, minced

1½ medium onions, finely chopped

1 small bay leaf

1 teaspoon dried oregano, crumbled

1 teaspoon hot red-pepper flakes

1½ teaspoons salt

½ teaspoon coarsely ground black pepper

¼ cup extra-virgin olive oil

1 green or red bell (or other fresh sweet) pepper, coarsely diced

2 tablespoons tomato paste

1½ cups dry red wine

1 28-ounce can diced tomatoes

1 cup bottled clam juice

1 cup chicken broth

1½ pounds mixed fish (bluegill and largemouth bass), cut in 2-inch pieces

½ pound large shrimp

1 pound clams or mussels, shells cleaned and de-bearded

¼ cup parsley, finely chopped

2 or 3 tablespoons finely chopped fresh basil

Cook first seven ingredients (through black pepper) in oil in a large, heavy pot over medium heat. Stir often, cooking until onions are softened. Add bell pepper and tomato paste, stirring until paste is well incorporated into mixture, a minute or so. Add wine and boil until reduced by half, about 5 minutes. Add tomatoes with their juices, clam juice and chicken broth. Cover and simmer for 25 to 30 minutes. Season with salt and pepper.

Add fish, shrimp and mussels to pot and simmer, covered, until fish is cooked through and mussel shells open, about 5 to 10 minutes. Remove bay leaf and any shellfish that didn't open. Stir in parsley and basil.

Serve in large soup bowls with ciabatta, a baguette or any sturdy, firm-crusted white bread for sopping up the broth. Fill your glasses with the rest of the red wine.

"The discovery of a new dish does more for human happiness than the discovery of a star."

—Jean-Anthelme Brillat-Savarin

I had almonds on hand when I made this, but I think pecans also would be tasty.

walleye encrusted
with breadcrumbs and almonds

Serves 2

1-pound walleye fillet
½ cup almonds
½ cup breadcrumbs
1 tablespoon unsalted butter, melted
2 tablespoons Dijon mustard
1 tablespoon parsley
2 tablespoons Parmigiano-Reggiano cheese, finely grated
1 tablespoon extra-virgin olive oil
Salt and freshly ground pepper

Preheat oven to 350°F. Generously oil a broiler pan and place fish in the pan flesh side up. Sprinkle with salt and pepper. In a food processor, mix nuts and breadcrumbs until nuts are finely chopped, and then transfer to a bowl. Mix in butter, mustard, parsley and cheese. Gently press the crumb mixture onto the fish, covering entire fillet on one side. Drizzle the olive oil over the fillet and bake until flesh is opaque.

Raise your oven rack and preheat broiler. Broil fish until crust is golden. Don't take your eyes off the fish while it is under the broiler. The crust browns rapidly, and—depending upon your broiler and the distance between the heat source and the fish—you should have a golden crust within a minute or two.

Serve the fish with lemon wedges and a quick sauce made with plain yogurt, fresh minced dill and a few squirts of fresh lemon juice. Accompany with new potatoes and fresh, edible-pod peas tossed together with fresh herbs and butter.

"It was in France that I first learned about food. And that even the selection of a perfect pear, a ripe piece of Brie, the freshest butter, the highest quality cream were as important as how the dish you were going to be served was actually cooked."

—Robert Carrier

If you've never made spring rolls, it may take a while to get the technique down. However, once you do, you'll want to make them over and over again with your own blend of ingredients. Add carrots one time, cabbage and chopped toasted peanuts the next. These were inspired by a favorite Vietnamese restaurant in St. Louis, which boasts the city's best spring rolls—and I can't argue with that. Fresh ingredients, light as a breeze, nutritious, low-cal, beautiful to look at—they are the near-perfect food. What's more, you don't feel any guilt after eating two pieces as an appetizer or four or five as a light meal. Dipping sauce is a must.

bass-and-crappie spring rolls

Serves 6 as an appetizer

8 ounces bass and/or crappie (trout works also)

Flour for light coating

2 to 3 tablespoons vegetable oil, just enough to lightly sauté the fish

1 ounce mung-bean threads (vermicelli noodles)

3 large Bibb or Boston lettuce leaves

12 6-inch-round rice papers, plus additional in case some tear

12 large Thai basil leaves

½ cup fresh cilantro, loosely packed

½ cup fresh mint leaves, loosely packed

1 small avocado, cut into 12 slices

¼ cup toasted peanuts, coarsely chopped

rolling in the mint and basil

I usually make these rolls in the summer and fall, when I have mint and several different kinds of basil (including Thai) growing in great abundance in my garden. However, you may purchase basil at Asian grocery stores, along with the bean threads, rice papers, rice vinegar and fish sauce.

Coat fish lightly in flour that has been seasoned with salt and pepper. Heat oil in medium-hot skillet and sauté fish until lightly browned on both sides. Set aside to cool.

In a bowl, soak bean threads in very hot water to cover. When they are soft, but still have a bit of a bite to them (about 10 minutes), drain well in a colander.

Cut out and discard ribs from lettuce leaves. Wash and dry thoroughly.

Break fish into 6 portions, and assemble rest of ingredients within easy reach.

In a shallow baking pan, soak 2 rounds of rice paper in warm water until very pliable, about 45 seconds. Meanwhile dampen two tea towels and spread one out on a flat work surface.

Carefully spread both soaked rice papers on the tea towel. Blot papers gently with the other towel. Arrange 1 piece of lettuce leaf on the bottom half of one paper, leaving a 1-inch border along the bottom edge. Cover lettuce with about ⅙ of the fish. On top of that place 2 basil leaves, side by side. Cover those with ⅙ each of bean threads, then cilantro, mint, avocado and peanuts.

Roll up filling tightly in rice paper, folding insides after first roll to completely enclose filling, and continue rolling. Wrap remaining rice paper around spring roll in same manner (double wrapping covers any tears and makes the roll more stable and easier to eat). Wrap roll in a rinsed and squeezed-dry tea towel. Make 5 more rolls with remaining ingredients in the same manner, covering each with towel as they are made.

Halve the rolls diagonally and serve with dipping sauce.

spring roll dipping sauce

½ cup sugar
½ cup rice vinegar
½ cup water
⅓ cup fish sauce
2 garlic cloves, minced
½ teaspoon minced fresh ginger root (peeled)
1½ teaspoons dried red pepper flakes
2 small sprigs cilantro, minced

Combine sugar, vinegar and water in a small saucepan. Heat to dissolve sugar. Once sugar is dissolved, remove pan from heat and add remaining ingredients. Stir well. Once cooled, this sauce will keep in the refrigerator for several days. Serve alongside spring rolls for dipping.

Leftover dipping sauce makes a wonderful dressing for Asian salads (see *Trout and Sprout Salad* on page 108).

I've long loved a recipe from my files for fresh okra with tomatoes. I make it every summer when both vegetables are at their peaks. I often had thought about adding fish to it, as well. One night I experimented with catfish and threw in some coconut, also, to play up the Afro-Caribbean food craving I was having. I love the lively combination of flavors and colors in the resulting dish—the zesty ginger, earthy red tomatoes and green okra, white fish, hot peppers and sweet coconut.

Caribbean catfish with okra and tomatoes

Serves 2

2 tablespoons extra-virgin olive oil

2 garlic cloves, chopped

1 1- by 2-inch piece fresh ginger, peeled and chopped

1 teaspoon minced fresh hot red pepper (or ¾ teaspoon dried hot red-pepper flakes)

2 large tomatoes, quartered

1 medium red bell pepper, chopped

¾ teaspoon salt

¼ teaspoon coarsely ground black pepper

½ pound small fresh okra, untrimmed

½ pound catfish, cut into 1- by 2-inch pieces

2 to 3 tablespoons grated fresh or dried coconut

2 cups cooked white rice

Heat olive oil in large skillet over medium heat. Put garlic and ginger in food processor and pulse until finely chopped. Add mixture to skillet with hot pepper and stir for a minute.

Add tomatoes, bell pepper, salt and black pepper to food processor and pulse 2 or 3 times until coarsely chopped. Add to skillet and cook over medium heat, stirring occasionally, for 10 minutes.

Stir in okra and simmer, covered, 4 or 5 minutes. Stir in catfish and coconut and cook, covered, 8 to 10 minutes or until tender.

Serve over a bed of hot rice.

"Food is, delightfully, an area of licensed sensuality, of physical delight which will, with luck and enduring taste buds, last our life long."

—Antonia Till

catfish
with lemon and pecans

2 catfish fillets, 6 to 8 ounces each

Salt

Freshly ground pepper

Flour for dredging

2 tablespoons vegetable oil

¼ cup pecans (whole or chopped)

3 tablespoons fresh lemon juice

1½ tablespoons unsalted butter

1 tablespoon finely chopped Italian parsley or fresh chives

Dry the fillets with paper towels, and season with salt and pepper. Dredge in flour and tap off excess.

Heat oil in a medium skillet, and when hot, place fillets in the skillet skin side up. Sauté fish until the first side is golden, about 5 minutes. Turn over fillets, reduce heat to medium, and continue cooking 3 or 4 minutes more until cooked through. Remove skillet from heat and place fish on a warm platter.

Add pecans to the same skillet and toast over low heat, stirring for about a minute until lightly browned.

Add the lemon juice and butter to the skillet and stir a few times. Turn off the heat and season the pecans with salt and pepper.

To serve, top the fillets with the pecan sauce and sprinkle with parsley or chives. Accompany with freshly sautéed spinach, oven-roasted potato chunks and *Opal's Cornbread*.

The subject of cornbread can cause heated debates between cooks from the north and those from the south. Southerners are adamant about flourless cornbread, and northerners tend to like theirs made with flour—more cakelike, it seems. I grew up in mid-Missouri, so I guess I could have gone either way, but I definitely prefer the flourless variety, just as my mother always made it—often with white cornmeal. An iron skillet preheated in the oven is requisite for the golden-perfection, crispy-lacy bottom crust.

Opal's cornbread

Makes 8 generous wedges of cornbread

4 teaspoons baking powder

1 teaspoon salt

2 cups coarsely ground yellow or white cornmeal

2 eggs

1 cup milk

¼ cup vegetable oil, plus 1 tablespoon

Preheat oven to 425°F. Sift baking powder and salt over a medium bowl. Stir in cornmeal and mix well. Set aside. In another bowl combine eggs, milk and ¼ cup oil; mix well. At this point, put a tablespoon of oil into a 12-inch cast-iron skillet and place in hot oven for a few minutes. Pour wet mixture into dry and gently stir to combine, taking care not to overbeat.

Carefully remove hot skillet from oven and tilt to coat bottom with the oil. Pour in cornbread mixture and listen to the sizzle! Return immediately to the oven and bake until golden, about 20 minutes. Test after 15 minutes with toothpick inserted in center. Remove from oven when a toothpick comes out clean.

Cut in wedges and try not to eat a whole piece before sitting down at the table.

catfish tacos with fresh-tomato salsa

1 pound catfish fillets
2 garlic cloves, minced
3 tablespoons fresh lime juice
Salt and coarsely ground pepper
4 to 6 6-inch corn tortillas
2 cups chopped Romaine lettuce
1 avocado, cubed
¼ cup feta cheese, crumbled

Bernadette's Fresh-Tomato Salsa

Place fish on lightly oiled, rimmed baking sheet. Mix garlic and lime juice and drizzle mixture over fish. Sprinkle with salt and pepper and let stand 15 minutes.

Broil fish in oven (you also may grill it) until opaque in center, 6 to 8 minutes. While fish is cooking, warm tortillas directly on a burner over lowest heat, turning once, until heated through. Watch carefully; the first side needs only 20 seconds or so, and the second side even less time. Alternatively, you may heat tortillas in a pan. Keep them warm in a tortilla basket lined with a cloth towel or napkin.

Cut fish into 1-inch pieces. Top each tortilla with lettuce, then fish. Drizzle with salsa and top with avocado and cheese. Serve with your favorite local ale.

Bernadette's fresh-tomato salsa   Makes about 4 cups of salsa

This makes enough to spice up a half dozen tacos, plus some left over to have with tortilla chips the next day. You can throw it together in the time it takes to have someone else prep the ingredients for the tacos.

4 to 5 garlic cloves, minced
1 fresh jalapeno pepper, minced
2 medium fresh sweet peppers (red, orange, yellow or green or combination), diced
½ to ¾ medium onion, diced
5 to 6 medium tomatoes (a variety of colors and types), diced
Several tablespoons finely chopped cilantro
Juice of fresh lime
Salt and coarsely ground pepper to taste

Combine all ingredients in a bowl and serve.

don't measure, just taste!

I never measure the ingredients for this salsa, and I suggest you don't either. Experiment with the quantities until you get the combination that tastes right for you. Always keep extra tomatoes on hand in case you need to add more to tone down the heat. I usually add the garlic and jalapeno sparingly if I'm serving people of whose tastes I'm uncertain. If I know everyone likes "hot" the way I do, I go whole hog and use lots of garlic and jalapeno. If fresh, local tomatoes are not in season, use canned. I love the chopped, fire-roasted varieties available in many grocery stores.

Among my cookbook collection is a tattered and splattered old notebook from a Chinese cooking class that I took back in the disco era. I pull it out every once in a while when I get a hankering for an old-school dish from my youth—cashew chicken or egg fu yung, for instance. In the class we made this with pork, but I've found that catfish takes to the sweet-and-sour treatment very well. Put on your *Saturday Night Fever* soundtrack and crank up the wok!

sweet-and-sour catfish

Serves 4

Catfish

1 pound catfish fillets

½ teaspoon salt

2 teaspoons soy sauce

2 teaspoons cornstarch

1 teaspoon dry sherry

Dash freshly
ground pepper

Vegetables and fruit

3 large carrots, cut into wedges
(See *Carrot-Cutting Tip*.)

1 sweet red bell pepper,
cut into 1-inch squares

¼ pound sugar snap peas
or snow peas

1 20-ounce can unsweetened
chunk pineapple in juice
(drain fruit, reserving juice)

1 large slice (about ¼-inch thick)
peeled fresh ginger root

1 tablespoon peanut oil

Sweet-and-sour sauce

⅔ cup pineapple juice

⅔ cup water

⅓ cup vinegar

¼ cup brown sugar

½ teaspoon salt

1 teaspoon soy sauce

1 teaspoon sweet pickle juice

2 tablespoons cornstarch
mixed with 4 tablespoons
water to form paste

Batter for fish

⅔ cup flour

⅓ cup cornstarch

Dash freshly
ground pepper

½ teaspoon salt

½ to ⅔ cup cold water

½ teaspoon
baking powder

Oil for deep frying

Cut fish into bite-sized chunks (about 1½-inch squares). Season with salt, soy sauce, cornstarch, sherry and pepper.

Prepare vegetables and fruit and set aside.

Combine first seven sauce ingredients (through pickle juice) and set aside. Make cornstarch paste and set aside.

Mix together first four batter ingredients and then add ½ cup water and stir. The consistency should be like that of pancake batter. If it's too thick, add remaining water. Just before frying, add the baking powder and stir.

Assemble all prepared ingredients, as well as a medium bowl, within close reach of the cooking element. Heat oil in wok for deep frying. Drop fish in batter and mix gently. Put fish pieces in hot oil one by one, a few pieces at a time, so as not to crowd. When golden brown, remove from oil. Drain on paper towels. Empty wok of oil and clean with paper towel.

Add peanut oil to wok; when hot, add ¼ teaspoon salt and ginger slice. Brown ginger slightly, then add carrots and sweet red pepper. Stir fry about 2 minutes, then add snow peas. Stir another minute and then remove all vegetables from wok to medium bowl. Remove ginger slice from vegetables. Add sauce to wok and turn heat to medium high. Thicken with cornstarch paste, adding slowly when liquid is at a full boil. As soon as sauce begins to thicken, add pineapple and cooked vegetables. Stir well and turn off heat. Add fish, stirring well to combine. Serve immediately with hot rice.

carrot-cutting tip

Peel carrots and trim ends. Make first cut a long diagonal about a ¼-inch thick. Rotate carrot a quarter turn and make another diagonal slice. Proceed with rest of carrots, turning and cutting into diagonal chunks—roughly triangular. Cutting them in this way gives the carrot chunks a nice heft, an interesting shape, and keeps them safer from overcooking.

Former longtime Conservation Department wildlife biologist, Dave Urich, fries the best catfish I've ever had. I don't eat much fried food anymore, but I'd expend my yearly allotment on a plate of Dave's catfish. I love the hint of tangy mustard between the moist fish and the crispy crust. The key to success, Dave says, is to cut all the fish into same-size pieces so they fry evenly and they're ready to be taken out at the same time.

Dave Urich's fried catfish

A mess of catfish
Yellow mustard for coating
Yellow corn meal for rolling
Peanut oil for frying

After you cut the fish into pieces, coat them in mustard; then roll them in yellow corn meal. Deep fry in peanut oil until golden and crispy.

trusty trotlines for a dependable catch

"Trotline fishing is the most dependable and probably the easiest way to catch big catfish out of our reservoirs and rivers," says Dave. "It's a lot of fun, too. I usually set my trotlines in about 10 feet of water and try to keep the lines 3 feet off the bottom. I run the lines between trees. For my main line, I use # 60, 580-pound test, nylon braid. Flatheads are found in submerged brush or old flooded trees, and you need line that won't break easily. If the hooks snag on the brush, I can wrap the line around a canoe paddle, brace the paddle on the inside of the boat and pull the hooks free using the boat motor. The line never breaks."

This dish resulted from a frustrating shopping experience that turned out for the best. One night I went to a local grocery to buy fish called for in the Chinese recipe I wanted to make for guests. They were to be at my house in less than 2 hours. "Won't have that until next week," said the clerk behind the fish counter. Desperate for a substitute, I plucked catfish from the plentiful supply in the case, and a new favorite was born.

catfish goes to China

Serves 2

2 catfish fillets, about 8-inch-long pieces

1 teaspoon salt

2 tablespoons cornstarch

2 tablespoons tamari or light soy sauce

2 tablespoons sesame oil

2 tablespoons dry sherry

2 tablespoons red-wine vinegar

2 teaspoons sugar

5 tablespoons vegetable oil

1 tablespoon coarsely chopped fresh
   ginger root (peeled)

4 green onions, chopped in ¼-inch slices

Place fish on a baking sheet and score them diagonally 3 times on each side. Rub both sides with the salt, and dust both sides with the cornstarch, inside the slashes also.

Combine soy sauce, sesame oil, sherry, vinegar and sugar in a small bowl. Set aside.

Heat a large, heavy skillet over high heat until quite hot. Add the vegetable oil, swirl and heat for 30 seconds. Add ginger and green onions and stir quickly until onions are bright green and aromatic. Push them to the side of the pan and slide in the fish. Brown for approximately 1 minute on each side. Turn the heat to low and fry each side 4 to 5 minutes until crisp and brown.

Stir sauce ingredients vigorously, turn heat back to high, and splash the sauce on top of fish, basting and turning them once as the sauce cooks.

Remove with a spatula to a hot serving dish; scrape ginger and onions on top of fish, but leave most of the oil in the pan.

presentation tip

Double the recipe to serve four, and present the fillets side by side atop rice on a pretty platter. Accompany with stir-fried spinach and mushrooms or stir-fried broccoli. A bean sprout salad with carrots also goes well.

water-to-rice ratio made easy

Forget measuring cups when trying to determine how much water to use to cook rice. I learned this wonderful technique from Chinese cookbook author Irene Kuo. I've been doing it this way for 25 years, and it hasn't failed me yet. Rinse rice until water runs clear; add rice to pan, leveling it out with your hand. Then, place your hand flat on the rice in the pot. Add water slowly, with other hand. When the water comes three-quarters of the way up your hand, the ratio is correct. Boil (hand removed) for 1 minute; then immediately turn heat to low. Cover and simmer for 20 minutes. Do not peek while it is cooking. Turn off heat and serve.

One late-April evening, I had a bit of catfish and asparagus I needed to use, and they both found their way into this tasty soup. It was the perfect light fare to end a beautiful spring day in the garden.

catfish-asparagus bisque

Serves 2 to 4

2 tablespoons butter

1 small onion, chopped

2 medium garlic cloves, chopped coarsely

1 small potato, cut into bite-sized pieces

1 tablespoon flour

1 32-ounce package organic, low-sodium chicken broth

1 pound asparagus, trimmed and cut into 1-inch pieces

½ pound catfish, cut into bite-sized chunks

½ fresh lemon, juiced

Salt to taste

½ teaspoon coarsely ground pepper

1 tablespoon minced fresh parsley

1 tablespoon minced fresh chives (optional)

Melt butter in medium saucepan over medium heat. Add onion, garlic and potato and cook until tender, stirring often for 8 to 10 minutes. Add flour and stir 2 more minutes. Gradually mix in broth and bring mixture to a boil.

Add asparagus pieces and simmer until asparagus is tender, about 10 to 15 minutes. Cool slightly. Purée mixture in manageable batches in the food processor or blender. Return puréed mixture to the saucepan.

Add catfish and lemon juice. Cover with lid, turn heat to medium low, and let fish poach in liquid for 8 to 12 minutes or until fork tender. Season to taste with salt and pepper. Ladle into soup bowls and sprinkle with parsley and chives.

trout with toasted-almond orange sauce

Fish

2 trout fillets
Vegetable oil
Salt and coarsely ground black pepper

Sauce

2 tablespoons unsalted butter
Juice of 3 oranges
Juice of ½ lemon
1 tablespoon orange zest

Garnish

2 tablespoons finely chopped parsley
2 tablespoons finely chopped prosciutto (optional)
¼ cup whole toasted almonds, cut in halves
Pomegranate seeds (optional)

Place fillets on an oiled baking sheet and brush them lightly with oil, salt and pepper.

Melt butter in a small saucepan, add juices and bring to a boil. Reduce the liquid until half its original volume. Remove from the heat and add the orange zest.

While sauce is reducing, broil fillets until the flesh is opaque (See *Canadian Cooking Theory* on page 106). Drizzle each fillet with the sauce. Sprinkle with parsley, prosciutto and nuts. If you have a pomegranate on hand, sprinkle on a few seeds along with the other garnishes.

Serve with garlic mashed potatoes and lightly cooked fresh spinach. A salad of Romaine lettuce, red grapefruit chunks and avocado slices dressed with vinaigrette also would go well.

"The secret of good cooking is, first, having a love of it… If you're convinced that cooking is drudgery, you're never going to be good at it, and you might as well warm up something frozen."

—James Beard

I have used this recipe for smoking all kinds of fish—catfish, trout, paddlefish and salmon. I credit two former Conservation Department employees, Pam Haverland and Joe Dillard, for passing it my way. Two large hickory trees in my yard provide twigs and bark for soaking.

smoked fish

Makes enough brine to smoke 4 pounds of fish, which fills 2 racks in an average-sized smoker.

Brine for soaking fish

2 quarts water

1 cup salt

⅓ cup brown sugar

¼ cup lemon juice

1 teaspoon finely chopped garlic

4 pounds fish

1 quart hickory wood chips or twigs

Mix thoroughly the first five ingredients (through garlic) and pour into a large rectangular ceramic or glass pan. Add fillets or whole fish to brine, making sure liquid covers them completely. Cover, chill and let soak 30 to 45 minutes. (Don't soak longer or you will risk the fish being too salty.)

Remove fish from brine (don't rinse) and put directly in smoker. Put thicker fish on top rack. Smoke approximately 1½ to 2 hours, until meat is flaky.

smoking tips

I use a very basic two-tiered charcoal smoker. I like to use the lump charcoal rather than briquettes. Light the charcoal after you put the fish in the brine. At the same time, put about a quart of hickory wood chips or twigs to soak in a pan or small bucket of water. When coals are ready, drain wood chips and add to the coals. Don't take the lid off the smoker during the first hour.

If you've always avoided sushi because you equate it with raw fish, give this one a try. These rolls (made with smoked trout, fresh raw vegetables and seasoned rice wrapped in seaweed) are delicious, nutritious and easy to make once you get the hang of it. Doing it once will give you the confidence—honest! Soon you'll love the challenge and order of making the various components, seeing all the gorgeous food colors side by side and the wonderful sensual experience of putting them all together. The resultant delectable little spirals will reward every minute of your efforts.

smoked-trout sushi

Makes 36 rolls

Dipping sauce

¼ cup soy sauce

¼ cup rice vinegar

2 teaspoons sugar

1 tablespoon chopped green onion or chives

2 teaspoons minced fresh ginger root (peeled)

½ teaspoon Asian sesame oil

¼ teaspoon chile oil

Sushi rice

2 cups short-grain rice (often called sushi rice)

⅓ cup rice vinegar

2 tablespoons mirin (sweet rice wine)

3 tablespoons sugar

1½ teaspoons salt

Roll filling

6 (8- by 7-inch) sheets roasted nori (dried seaweed)

¼ cup wasabi paste

¼ cup toasted sesame seeds

12 (¼- by 3½-inch) strips red bell pepper

12 (¼- by 3½-inch) strips peeled cucumber

12 (¼- by 3½-inch) strips carrot

12 thin slices avocado

12 (¾- by 3½-inch) slices smoked trout, skin removed (See *Smoked Fish* on page 97.)

Pickled ginger

sushi mat substitute

If you don't have a bamboo sushi mat, some sushi makers say that a kitchen towel or a piece of wax paper will work equally well.

Sushi rolls can be prepared a day in advance. Wrap them individually in plastic wrap and refrigerate. Bring to room temperature before serving.

Preparing the dipping sauce

Combine soy sauce, vinegar and ¼ cup water in a small saucepan and bring to a boil. Remove from the heat and stir in remaining sauce ingredients. Cover and set aside while preparing the rice.

Preparing the rice

Place rice in fine-mesh strainer and wash with cold water until water runs clear. Drain well. In medium saucepan over medium-high heat, combine rice and 2 cups water. Bring to a boil, reduce heat to low and cover. Simmer until water is absorbed, about 20 minutes. Turn off heat and let the rice rest, covered, for a few minutes.

Transfer the hot rice to a large mixing bowl. Combine the vinegar, mirin, sugar and salt in a small bowl. Stir until the sugar and salt are dissolved. Gradually add the vinegar mixture to the rice, mixing well by using a slashing (rather than circular) motion across the rice with a flat wooden spoon. Cover the bowl with a damp cloth and let the rice cool. Meanwhile, gather the remaining filling ingredients within easy reach of where you will be assembling the rolls.

Assembling the rolls

Place sushi mat on a cutting board with slats running crosswise. Place a nori sheet on the mat, lining up the long edge of the sheet with the edge of the mat nearest you. Moisten the nori by dabbing it with a wet cloth. Lightly moisten hands with water, then gently spread one sixth of the rice onto the nori sheet in an even layer, leaving a 2-inch border on the long end opposite you.

Spread ½ teaspoon wasabi paste in a thin horizontal line across the middle of the rice. Sprinkle 2 teaspoons of the sesame seeds over all. Arrange 2 strips of each vegetable and 2 avocado slices in a line across the bottom of the rice. Top vegetable strips with 2 slices of trout.

Beginning with edge nearest you, lift mat up with thumbs, holding filling in place with fingers, and fold mat over filling. Squeeze gently but firmly along length of roll and tug top edge of mat away from you to tighten. (Nori border will still be visible below top edge of mat.) Open mat and roll log forward ¼ turn, then fold mat over again and squeeze gently but firmly to seal nori border. If the top is a little dry, moisten with water before rolling over it to seal the sushi. Place the completed roll on a platter and cover with wax paper and a light towel. Repeat to form remaining rolls.

With a slightly moistened very sharp knife, trim ends off the rolls and save them for snacking later. Cut each roll into 1-inch rounds. Serve with soy dipping sauce, slices of pickled ginger and remaining wasabi paste.

where do I get all this stuff?

Sushi mats, pickled ginger, wasabi, mirin, chile oil, sesame oil, rice vinegar and seaweed are all available in Asian grocery stores and in many American grocery stores that have sections devoted to foods from other cultures. There are many products called wasabi, but look for the "real wasabi" without food coloring and other additives. When shopping for sesame oil, make sure what you are buying is toasted. In my shopping experience, when buying sesame oil at an Asian grocery store, I am most likely to find the toasted variety—even though it doesn't say so on the label. A time or two I have bought sesame oil in American grocery stores that turned out not to be toasted. The flavor is entirely different. Until I did a little research and discovered that sesame oil used in some other food cultures is not toasted, I was perplexed.

This dish celebrates the marriage of bright green spring vegetables and the rosy hue of smoked trout. The fresh lemon juice and briny capers add a perfect counterpoint to the smokiness of the fish. If you're fortunate enough to have hickory nuts on hand, throw some in; they add a crunchy and earthy bonus. If you smoke the trout a day or two in advance, you can put this dish together in no time. I have hickory trees in my yard, and use the windfall twigs to add to the coals when smoking.

bowties with smoked trout and spring vegetables

Serves 2

½ pound bowtie or penne pasta

½ pound smoked trout (See *Smoked Fish* on page 97.)

¼ cup Parmigiano-Reggiano cheese, freshly grated

1 small lemon, zest and juice

2 tablespoons hickory nuts or pecans, toasted briefly (optional, but recommended)

½ pound asparagus, cut into 2-inch pieces

¼ cup freshly shelled peas

1 tablespoon extra-virgin olive oil

1 heaping teaspoon capers, drained

Salt

Coarsely ground black pepper

While pasta boils, break trout into largish bite-sized pieces and prep other ingredients (grate cheese, zest and juice lemon, toast nuts).

Two or 3 minutes before pasta is ready, steam the asparagus briefly in a covered pan with a small amount of water; throw the peas into the pan with the asparagus during the last minute of cooking. Be sure to keep a close watch on the vegetables. The asparagus and the peas need to retain their bright green color and still offer a nice firm bite when ready to add to the pasta. Drain well before adding to pasta.

Drain pasta, retaining a tablespoon or so of the water in which it was cooked. Place pasta, and the retained cooking water, into a serving bowl. Toss with the olive oil, capers, salt, pepper and the remaining ingredients. Serve with a Chardonnay, Sauvignon Blanc or any dry white wine.

"You don't have to cook fancy or complicated masterpieces—just good food from fresh ingredients."

—Julia Child

I often build cold winter evenings around impromptu soups, made from whatever is on my kitchen counter and in the fridge. Leftover trout I had smoked a few days earlier found a home in this hearty little chowder one December evening.

smoked trout chowder

Serves 4

2 tablespoons extra-virgin olive oil

1 medium onion, finely diced

3 carrots, finely diced

2 medium potatoes, finely diced

2 stalks celery, finely diced

1 quart chicken broth

¼ cup cream or milk

¼ pound smoked trout, broken into bite-sized pieces (See *Smoked Fish* on page 97.)

Handful of fresh spinach, finely chopped

A few fresh dill sprigs, finely chopped (pinch of dried is okay if fresh not available)

Smoked Spanish paprika, a few pinches or to taste

Salt and freshly ground pepper

Sauté vegetables except spinach in oil about 10 minutes, stirring often. Add chicken broth and simmer, covered, until vegetables are very tender, about 45 minutes.

With a manual potato masher, mash vegetables in pot until chowder thickens to your satisfaction. (Alternatively, pour half of soup into a blender and process on low speed, taking care to press firmly on the lid with your hand during processing to prevent hot liquid from flying out of the top. Blend until thickened, then return contents to the pot and stir until well combined.)

Add cream, trout and spinach. Cook briefly until fish is heated through, but spinach still bright green. Season with dill, paprika, salt and pepper to taste. Serve immediately with good bread.

ready-made chicken broth

Nothing beats homemade chicken broth or stock, and it is great to have a supply in the freezer. However, I often use the ready-made variety, and always have several boxes of organic, free-range broth in my pantry. It comes in very handy for quick soups such as this one.

thickening tip

If, for whatever reason, a soup or chowder turns out a little too thin for your liking, thicken it up quickly with grated vegetables. I hold a grater over the pot as I shred a potato or carrot directly into the soup. Stir, pop on the lid and let cook another 10 minutes or so until the desired consistency is achieved.

The inspiration for these cakes comes from my dear friend, Michel Gregory, with whom I used to cook in Portland, Oregon. A native Northwesterner who has an exemplary culinary touch, Michel makes the best Dungeness crab cakes on the West Coast. I've substituted trout in this adaptation, and was thrilled with the result. The little cakes make an elegant first course or a nice light meal for two or three people.

Missouri "crab" cakes

Makes 8 or 9 two-inch cakes

1 cup trout (leftover from a previous grilling)
1 cup breadcrumbs (See *Make Your Own Crumbs*.)
4 tablespoons freshly grated Parmigiano-Reggiano cheese
2 green onions, chopped finely
1 heaping tablespoon finely chopped cilantro or parsley
1 heaping teaspoon finely chopped fresh hot red pepper
Juice of one small, fresh lemon
1 egg
A few pinches of salt and freshly ground
    black pepper to taste
2 tablespoons unsalted butter

Fresh mixed salad greens
Fresh Citrus-Vinaigrette Dressing

Mix trout well with ¼ cup of the breadcrumbs and the next seven ingredients (through salt and pepper). Mixture will be moist. Form into 2-inch patties. Dip patties in remaining crumbs and compress all over. Fry in butter over medium heat, cooking until bottom side is golden brown. Carefully turn and brown the other side.

Toss salad greens with small amount of vinaigrette dressing. Place on small oval dishes and top with three cakes.

make your own crumbs
Making your own bread crumbs is easy. Plus, they're tastier and less expensive than what you can buy. Cube good, coarsely textured white bread and dry in a 325°F oven; then chop finely in the food processor. Freeze any extra crumbs.

Michel's Napa-cabbage slaw with green apples

You may prefer, instead of the salad greens, to serve the trout cakes with this easy and delicious slaw.

½ head Napa cabbage (Chinese or celery cabbage), outer leaves only
1 green apple
Several sprigs of cilantro, finely chopped
1 lime or Meyer lemon, freshly squeezed
Salt to taste

Stack cabbage leaves and cut in thin chiffonade (long, thin strips); then cut leaves in half.

Cut unpeeled apple into julienne slices. Toss cabbage and apple in a bowl with cilantro, citrus juice and salt.

fresh citrus-vinaigrette dressing

Extra-virgin olive oil
Citrus juice (lemon, orange or grapefruit)
Fresh garlic, finely chopped
Salt and pepper

Mix approximately three parts oil to one part juice. Add a touch of garlic and whisk. Season to taste with salt and pepper and whisk again. To test, dip a piece of lettuce in the dressing and amend to suit your taste.

a crime against lettuce

Of all the culinary sins committed in restaurants (and at home), nothing irks me more than to be served a green salad soaked in dressing. What I want most in a fresh salad is to taste the brightness and freshness of the greens, not a dressing "soup"—no matter how interesting it is. Err on the side of underdressing your salads. You always can add more olive oil or vinegar, but you can't undo a soggy salad.

105

Fire up the grill on one of those hot summer days, when tomatoes and basil are abundant at the farmers market or in your garden. Locally cured bacon makes this dish superb.

grilled trout stuffed with tomato and basil

Serves 2 to 4

2 whole trout (cleaned, boned and butterflied)

Extra-virgin olive oil

Salt and freshly ground pepper

1 medium red, dead-ripe tomato, sliced

8 large fresh basil leaves

2 tablespoons freshly grated
   Parmigiano-Reggiano cheese

4 slices bacon

Rinse well both sides of fish and pat dry with a paper towel. On a baking sheet, place fish skin-side down, opening them flat like a book. Drizzle a teaspoon or so of olive oil over flesh of trout and rub in the oil. Sprinkle with salt and pepper. Place two slices of tomato on one half of the trout, topping each slice with two basil leaves. Sprinkle the length of the trout with 1 tablespoon cheese.

Fold unadorned side of the fish over the other side and wrap the whole fish in a spiral fashion with bacon; two bacon slices secure a medium-sized trout nicely. Repeat procedure with the other fish. Grill or broil in oven until bacon begins to crisp and trout is cooked through.

Side dishes that accompany nicely include fresh whole new potatoes; corn on the cob; green beans; cucumber, onion and sweet red-pepper rings in an herby vinaigrette; and crusty white bread. A glass of Pinot Grigio or Pinot Bianco doesn't hurt either.

Canadian cooking theory

I swear by the Canadian Cooking Theory for cooking fish, and have used it all my cooking life to determine when fish are done. First publicized by the Department of Fisheries of Canada, the basic principle is that fish can be cooked, no matter how, at 10 minutes per inch. The technique works with whole fish, steaks and fillets, and it applies to baking, braising, broiling, frying, poaching, sautéing, grilling, steaming and any other cooking method you can dream of. Measure your portion of fish at its thickest part (its depth, not across the fish), and calculate 10 minutes of cooking time for each inch of thickness. Having said all that, however, it is best to err on the side of undercooking. Some people prefer their fish on the rarer side, so always inquire of your guests' preferences.

cooking tip

A fish griller is perfect for this because it allows easy turning of the fish on the grill. If using a broiler, make sure fish is at least 5 inches from the broiler element.

This dish was another spontaneous invention after darkness forced me in from weed pulling in my garden one spring evening. It was 8:45, and I was hungry, but I didn't have anything in mind to eat. I opened up my fridge, examined the contents, and was eating a tasty little meal by 9 p.m. The farmers market trip two days before provided all the ingredients, save for the dressing. I had on hand a bag of crunchy bean sprouts, spinach, cilantro, a green onion, some garlic tops and some of my own mixed greens. Fresh trout was left over from weekend grilling.

trout and sprout salad

Serves 1 to 20 depending upon how much trout you have

Leftover grilled or baked trout, broken into bite-sized pieces

Fresh spinach

Mixed lettuces

Bean sprouts

Cilantro

Green onion

Garlic tops (the green tops of fresh garlic) or freshly minced garlic

Soy sauce

Sesame oil

Rice wine vinegar

I tossed the trout together with all the vegetables, a little soy, toasted sesame oil and rice wine vinegar. It was perfect! You also could add such things as peanuts, mung-bean threads and avocado. Fresh orange sections, carrots, red peppers or cucumbers come to mind, as well.

leftover serendipity

Leftover dipping sauce from the *Bass-and-Crappie Spring Rolls* (page 86) makes a wonderful dressing for this salad. Use leftover trout and other ingredients from the rolls here, as well.

"If you want to lose weight, don't buy a diet book; learn how to cook. When you do, a new world of delicious, nutritious and fulfilling dishes will open up to you and change how you eat, think about food and, ultimately, how you look." —BCD

It was at a trattoria in Venice where I fell in love—with sarde in saor, that is. The classic Venetian dish (made with fresh sardines marinated in onions, vinegar, pine nuts and golden raisins) made me obsessed with trying to find a way to enjoy a similar taste sensation in mid-Missouri. Trout stands in for sardines in this recipe and is a pretty impressive understudy.

trout in saor
(trout in the style of Venice)

Serves 4 as a first course

1 pound trout fillets
½ cup flour
¼ cup vegetable oil
Salt
2½ tablespoons extra-virgin olive oil
1 onion, sliced
¾ cup red-wine vinegar
1 teaspoon sugar
Pinch cinnamon
Pinch freshly ground black pepper
¼ cup pine nuts, toasted
¼ cup golden raisins, soaked in lukewarm water
Parsley and lemon slices for garnishing, if desired

Wash and dry fillets; dredge in flour to coat well on both sides. Fry fish in very hot vegetable oil until crisp and golden, turning once. Place on paper towels and season with salt.

Drain remaining vegetable oil from skillet and clean the pan with a paper towel. Lower heat to medium. Pour in olive oil, and, when heated, fry onion until translucent. Stir in vinegar, sugar, cinnamon and pepper. Boil for a minute or so, then remove from heat.

Arrange fillets in 2 layers in a glass dish, scattering pine nuts, drained raisins and onion mixture atop each layer. Marinate in the refrigerator for at least 24 hours. Serve at room temperature as an appetizer or first course.

"I don't understand when Americans say, 'I don't have time to cook.' To me that is like saying 'I don't have time to take a shower.'"

—Marcella Hazan

Brook Harlan—chef and culinary arts educator at the Columbia Area Career Center—invokes the Creole soul of New Orleans and the haute cuisine of its French heritage for this tasty treatment of crawfish. He did a stint in the kitchen of the venerable Commander's Palace in New Orleans, which puts on some pretty lavish cocktail parties from time to time. He recalled one of his favorite hors d'oeuvres from those days and reinterpreted it here with a zesty crawfish filling encased in a delicate pastry shell.

crawfish vol-au-vent

Makes 25 to 30 hors d'oeuvres

Filling

1½ pounds crawfish

2 tablespoons oil

1 garlic clove, minced

½ onion, small diced

1 celery stalk, small diced

4 mushrooms, small diced

½ bell pepper, small diced

1 tablespoon flour

¼ cup cream

½ cup crawfish, shrimp or chicken stock

½ teaspoon cayenne pepper (more for spicier filling)

1 teaspoon paprika

1 teaspoon dried oregano or 2 teaspoons fresh

3 tablespoons sherry

Salt, pepper and Worcestershire sauce to taste

Pastry shells

2 sheets of puff pastry (available in the frozen-food section of many grocery stores)

1 egg, beaten

10 chives, sliced for garnish

Preparing the crawfish

Rinse crawfish thoroughly and boil them in lightly salted water for a few minutes. Remove from the water and let cool slightly. To remove the tail meat, twist the body and tail in opposite directions. Peel the first couple of knuckles (sections) off the top part of the tail. Place your thumb in the middle of the tail fan; press firmly and pull the meat out of the tail. Repeat as necessary until you have four ounces of tail meat. (Crawfish yield about 15 percent meat, so 1½ pounds of cooked whole crawfish should yield 4 ounces.) Dice the tails finely and set aside.

Making the crawfish filling

Heat oil in sauté pan. Add garlic, onion, celery, mushrooms and bell pepper, and sauté for a few minutes. Add flour and stir to create a roux. When the flour is light golden brown, slowly stir in cream and stock until well mixed. Simmer until mixture has thickened and flour taste has cooked out. Add crawfish tails, cayenne, paprika and oregano; simmer until crawfish are opaque. Finish with sherry and season with salt, pepper and Worcestershire. Set aside and reheat gently before filling pastry shells.

Making the pastry shells

Thaw puff pastry as per package instructions. Unfold thawed pastry sheets and brush top of one with beaten egg. Place another sheet on top and brush with beaten egg. Cut double-stacked puff pastry into even (approximately 2-inch) strips, then cut into squares or diamonds. With a sharp paring knife, cut each square through the first layer only—just inside and all the way around the perimeter of each square or diamond. Make sure your cut is far enough away (about ⅛ inch) from the edge, so the pastry wall will be stable. (The purpose here is to create a future cavity, which later will be filled with the crawfish mixture. After the pastries are baked, the inside pieces will be lifted out and used as lids.)

Place shells about 1 inch apart on sheet pan lined with parchment paper. Brush each with beaten egg, and bake at 400°F until golden (about 12 to 15 minutes). They will double or triple in height. Remove the pastry lids and deepen the insides with your fingers or the handle of a spoon. Spoon crawfish mixture into the pastries as soon as possible, then cover with pastry lids. Garnish with sliced chives and serve.

N eighbor Gunilla Murphy and her husband, Dave, bring back a nice haul of crayfish every summer from Table Rock Lake near Branson. Gunilla's favorite way to cook them is as it is traditionally done in her native Sweden. "The Swedes are obsessed with crayfish," she says, "and every August (when they are most abundant), it is customary to have crayfish parties everywhere." Gunilla boils the crustaceans as soon as they get home from the lake and prepares them in the following way.

Swedish-style boiled crayfish
(kokta kräftor)

Serves 4

2 pounds crayfish (about 25)
2¾ quarts water
⅓ cup salt
Lots of fresh dill crowns

Transport the crayfish to your kitchen in an ice-filled cooler. Before cooking, make sure all the crayfish are alive. Bring the water, salt and dill to a boil. Add all the crayfish at once. After the water has returned to a boil, boil for 10 to 12 minutes. Let the crayfish cool in the liquid.

It works very well to freeze the crayfish in the liquid. When you are ready to eat them, defrost and serve very cold. They are delicious with crusty white bread and cheese. Aquavit and beer are the traditional Swedish beverages to accompany the crayfish, but Gunilla advises white wine also works well.

Missouri's freshwater crustaceans

Missouri is home to 35 species of crayfish and many are good to eat. Missouri anglers can legally harvest 150 of them daily with a fishing license. Our longpincered crayfish (left) is among the largest crayfish in North America, and they are numerous enough in the state to provide quite a feast. This species, which can have a body 6 inches long with pincers almost as long as its body, is believed to be indigenous only to the White River basin of southern Missouri and northern Arkansas. People who visit Table Rock Lake are finding that the reservoir holds an excellent population of large crayfish, and more and more anglers are harvesting them—and having fun doing it.

a cautionary note

Always make sure any crayfish you intend to eat is fully cooked. *Never* eat them raw.

113

Salad Niçoise is one of my favorite summer patio meals, and I never tire of it. I take great liberties with the traditional French recipe (made with tuna)—changing it up every time I make it with different fish and vegetables. I use whatever is fresh and seasonal or whatever is in the fridge that needs eating. It calls to me in late spring during asparagus and new potato season, and I make it every few weeks until the last green beans have been picked in early fall. Beautiful green vegetables are a visual and gustatory must in this composed salad. Consequently, asparagus or edible-pod peas in late spring give way to young, slender green beans in summer. Add another six or eight vegetables of varying colors, textures and shapes (new potatoes are requisite). Sweet corn in July sits in for button mushrooms earlier in the year and dead-ripe tomatoes replace avocados.

smoked paddlefish Niçoise

Serves 4

Salad

2 pounds smoked paddlefish or trout, cut into bite-sized pieces (See *Smoked Fish* on page 97.)

½ pound green beans, cooked (or another green vegetable such as asparagus or edible-pod peas)

12 small new potatoes, cooked

20 cherry tomatoes or other tomatoes

3 ears fresh corn, cooked and cut off cob

8 small beets, red or golden, cooked

12 calamata olives

2 hard-cooked eggs, quartered

1 medium red onion, sliced

¼ cup finely chopped fresh parsley (also chives and basil, if available)

Optional: avocado, mushrooms, sweet red or yellow bell pepper

Lemon vinaigrette

1 large lemon

Extra-virgin olive oil

Garlic

Salt and freshly ground pepper

Lemon zest

A couple of hours before serving, I usually steam all the vegetables that need cooking, let them cool and then cut them just before composing them on the platter.

To compose, place fish in center of platter and surround it with vegetables, keeping each in separate groups. Stud the display with olives and eggs, arrange red onion slices over all and sprinkle with parsley. Minutes before serving, generously drizzle lemon vinaigrette over all.

Serve with chunks of crusty bread and your favorite summer white wine.

"Learn to eat with the seasons; enjoy local foods when they're most abundant and delicious. After you've tasted local heirloom tomatoes in all their glorious shapes, colors and sizes, you'll never be able to buy another rock-hard, anemic tomato shipped from 1,000 miles away in December."

—BCD

Hickory nuts, black walnuts and pecans

hickory nuts, black walnuts and pecans
three nuts; endless culinary possibilities

Missouri's 149 native tree species are important food sources for its wildlife. Many birds, mammals and insects depend upon the trees' nuts, fruits, seeds, twigs and leaves for survival. The nuts of several of these trees also enhance the daily diets of the state's human population. Creative cooks throughout Missouri include native black walnuts, pecans and hickory nuts in their favorite dishes.

hickory nuts

I love and use all these nuts, but I have a particular fondness for hickory nuts. As a child, I spent hours hammering their rock-hard shells on an old chunk of railroad track, which was perfect for the job. My mother and I then would pry out the small pieces from the intricate cavities with nut picks. She'd use them a few weeks later inside her densely rich Christmas applesauce cake, which she'd top with caramel icing and pecans halves. Hickory nuts also are superb in savory dishes.

I have two trees in my yard, but the squirrels get the best nuts every year. What they leave me, instead, are hundreds of buried nuts, whose sprouts I must pluck annually from my gardens. Fewer and fewer places sell hickory nuts commercially, it seems, so I was delighted when I ran into Joe Holterman at a local farmers market.

Holterman (left) has been eating shellbark hickory nuts from the same tree since he was a child. He grew up on his family's Osage County farm near Westphalia, and still lives there today. He says shellbark hickories thrive in the bottomland soils of the Maries, Osage and Moreau rivers. He and his wife have been selling the sweet meats from the large nuts for 30 years at the Cole County Farmers Market. They also sell black walnuts and pecans from their farm and use a 50-year-old walnut cracker to open the shells. Mrs. Holterman, who uses hickory nuts in her cookies and cinnamon rolls, says that when their children were growing up, they preferred the nuts to any other.

black walnuts

Black walnut trees, in addition to being fine ornamentals due to their shape and large leaves, also produce deliciously rich nuts. They are found throughout the state. In fact, Missouri has more black walnut trees than any other state and is home to one of the world's largest suppliers of black-walnut food products.

pecans

Pecans thrive throughout the southeastern United States, but also grow in Missouri's rich, moist, bottomland soils. Missouri is located on the northern limits of pecan growing, but many pecan enthusiasts find our nuts unrivaled in sweetness. Though smaller than southern pecans, Missouri varieties have a higher oil content, which is desirable for ice cream and candy making.

plant your own nut trees

Black walnut and pecan seedlings may be purchased from the Missouri Department of Conservation's George O. White State Forest Nursery near Licking. The nursery offers Missouri residents a variety of seedlings for reforestation, windbreaks and erosion control, as well as for wildlife food and cover. For ordering information, visit *mdc.mo.gov*.

Nuts from shellbarks dwarf those from shagbarks, but both are delicious. The shellbark hickory is becoming rather scarce because it grows in rich, deep soils in river bottoms, many of which have been cleared to grow crops. Holterman says shellbark hickories yield nuts about 10 to 12 years after being planted; so, if your land has the right growing conditions, I'd say run— don't walk—to plant a few of these underappreciated Missouri treasures. You will have a good chance of being rewarded with the magnificently sweet nuts for the rest of your life.

some nutty tips

Select clean, unshelled nuts free from splits, cracks and holes. Nuts in their shells should be heavy for their size, indicating a fresh, meaty kernel. Nutmeats that rattle in their shells are usually stale.

Rich in oil, nuts quickly become rancid or stale if not stored properly. Store unshelled nuts in airtight containers in a cool, dry, dark location below 70°F.

Although unshelled nuts take up more room, they have a longer shelf life than shelled nuts. Additionally, whole, shelled nutmeats remain fresh longer than nuts in pieces—so chop nuts just before you use them.

Unsalted nuts keep longer than salted nutmeats. For long-term storage, package unshelled or shelled nuts in moisture/vapor-proof containers and store in the refrigerator or freezer; the lower the storage temperature, the longer the shelf life.

Nutty tips courtesy of University of Missouri Extension, Missouri Department of Agriculture and Missouri Northern Pecan Growers.

These not-so-sweet, nutritious muffins are wonderfully malleable and forgiving of just about anything you put in the batter. Add a few leftover nuts here, a handful of raisins or dried fruit there, or substitute rolled oats or wheat for part of the flour. You also can use whole wheat flour instead of white or varying proportions of each. I've even used part cornmeal. Sometimes I throw in flax, chia or sesame seeds.

Bernadette's catch-all muffins

Makes about 20 muffins

1½ cups sugar

2⅓ cups flour

2½ teaspoons baking soda, sifted

½ teaspoon salt

½ cup oil

2 eggs

2 cups buttermilk

1 cup boiling water

3 cups wheat bran

1 cup golden raisins (or part dried
   cranberries, dates or figs)

1 cup pecans or hickory nuts
   (toasted lightly, preferably)

Blend together first four ingredients (through salt) in one bowl and next three ingredients (oil through buttermilk) in another. Then, gently mix all seven together.

Meanwhile, pour water over bran and fruit in a separate bowl; let stand a few minutes, then stir and gently combine with the batter. Stir in nuts. Pour into medium-sized muffin tins lined with paper cups. (Batter also will keep in refrigerator for at least a week.)

Bake in a 400°F oven for 15 to 20 minutes or until a toothpick inserted in muffin's center comes out clean. Turn muffins onto a rack to cool.

no buttermilk? no worry.

When a recipe calls for buttermilk, I use a shortcut if I don't have any on hand and don't want to make a special trip to get some: I add a healthy squeeze of fresh lemon juice or a couple of teaspoons of apple cider vinegar to a cup of regular milk.

My mother's family recipe for oatmeal cookies has one of the oddest recipe methods I've encountered in five decades of cooking. It calls for mixing in baking powder, salt and baking soda at the end of the recipe—adding them one at a time, mixing well each time—to the heavy, lumpy batter. Although this makes it tougher to evenly distribute the leavening ingredients, I always do it this way, for sentimental reasons I guess. I usually progress from a big whisk through the coconut, to a wooden spoon with the nuts, to finally using my hands to incorporate the leavening ingredients. The mixture goes together quickly and bakes up into a crunchy, rich cookie—with which you can raise and lower your cholesterol at the same time! I made these for my dad all his life from the time I was 8 years old. I still can see him reclining in his easy chair with a handful of these in one hand and his newspaper in the other.

Mom's oatmeal cookies
with hickory nuts

Makes about 5 dozen cookies

2 eggs
2 cups brown sugar
1 cup melted butter
1 cup coconut
1 cup chopped hickory nuts
2 cups flour
4 cups rolled oats
1 teaspoon baking powder
Pinch of salt
½ teaspoon baking soda dissolved
   in 4 tablespoons of hot water

Preheat oven to 350°F. Beat eggs together and add other ingredients in order given. Mix well each time.

Roll mixture into 1½- to 2-inch balls and drop onto a cookie sheet, keeping them at least 2 inches apart. Tap each down with your fingers until slightly flattened, but retaining some roundness.

Bake 15 or 20 minutes until golden brown on the bottoms. They will harden as they cool.

Needless to say, they must be accompanied by a glass of milk or strong black coffee.

"Through careful observation and in-depth investigation, I've discovered that food uniquely defines our home, describes our heritage, and predicts our future."

—Melinda Hemmelgarn

This is a quick little dish to whip up when you don't have much time, but need a hearty and lively bit of protein. It makes a good side dish when the beans have been heated before being tossed with the remaining ingredients. It's also good with the beans at room temperature and served atop a freshly tossed green salad as a light main course. I cooked a variety of heirloom dried beans for this, but when time doesn't allow, canned ones work well, also. The sweet wildness of the hickory nuts complements the rustic beans.

beans with hickory nuts and feta

Serves 2 to 4

2 cups canned or freshly cooked brown, navy or cannellini beans

2 tablespoons finely chopped fresh parsley

2 tablespoons finely chopped sweet yellow or red pepper

2 to 3 tablespoons finely chopped red onion

3 tablespoons feta cheese, crumbled

1 to 2 garlic cloves, minced

2 tablespoons coarsely chopped hickory nuts or pecans

Salt and freshly ground pepper to taste

Extra-virgin olive oil and vinegar or lemon juice to taste

Rinse and drain beans. Toss with the rest of the ingredients.

change the spices, change the country

For another variation on this dish, try green or brown lentils (photo at right) with hickory nuts, pecans or black walnuts, or a combination of nuts. Change the longitude of the dish with the seasonings you choose. For a Mexican flair, you could add cumin, cilantro, fresh lime juice, tomato, jalapeno and avocado; serve with tortillas.

If you prefer a hint of India, then season the beans with turmeric, cinnamon, cayenne, cumin, fresh lemon and minced fresh ginger. Serve with naan. This is equally delicious as a leftover; just heat and serve over a bed of rice.

Here's a quick and deliciously rich pasta sauce that can be put together in less than 15 minutes. The sauce involves no heating and just a bit of chopping, grating and stirring. It was a favorite with customers at Pasta Cucina, a Portland, Oregon pasta shop where I once cooked. There we used filberts and English walnuts, but hickory nuts and pecans are wonderful substitutes in Missouri. As well as a glorious match for pasta, this sauce is fantastic as a light cloaking for steamed Brussels sprouts.

pasta with autumn nut sauce

Serves 4 as a main dish or 8 as a first course

1 pound dried pasta shells (whole-wheat or white)

Sauce
⅓ cup hickory nuts, coarsely chopped
⅓ cup pecans, coarsely chopped
3 garlic cloves, minced
⅓ cup Romano cheese, finely grated
⅓ cup Parmigiano-Reggiano cheese, finely grated
¾ teaspoon marjoram
3 tablespoons unsalted butter, melted
¾ cup cream
Salt and freshly ground pepper to taste

Cook pasta while composing sauce. Combine sauce ingredients in order given, stirring well after each addition. Add salt and pepper to taste.

Drain pasta in colander and add sauce to hot pot in which pasta has been cooked. Stir well, add pasta and stir again until well combined. Serve immediately.

the right pasta for the right sauce

Of all the glories of cooking and eating Italian food, none is more enjoyable to me than the endless variety of pasta shapes and sizes. Centuries of Italian creative genius are responsible for hundreds of shapes of dried and freshly made pasta. Choosing the right pasta shape to go with the right sauce is a particular preoccupation of Italians and of those who revere Italy's cuisine. Much has been written about it in venerable Italian cookbooks throughout the years, so I won't go into it here. Suffice it to say that conchiglie (shells), with their deep little cavities, are the perfect partners to cradle the nutty nuggets in this sauce.

My favorite dried pasta is produced by artisanal Italian pasta makers. It often is made with organic wheat grown on family farms, and extruded through bronze dies (which create a rough texture on the pasta that helps the sauce cling to it). Fortunately, the popularity of this carefully made dried pasta is increasing in the United States. As a result, it is available in many grocery stores that carry a good variety of Italian foods.

toasting nuts enhances flavor

In their raw state, our native nuts are delicious. However, I've found that a light toasting in a dry skillet or in the oven makes them even more wonderful. While certainly not necessary in this dish, toasting the nuts will make this sauce even better. Try it both ways to see which you prefer.

No pasta dish says autumn quite like this one, with its beautiful orange chunks of sweet roasted squash and toasted nuggets of freshly picked hickory nuts or pecans. It also can be dressed up or down depending upon your mood or whether you can afford the calories. Be sparing with the oil and butter, or go hog wild and add a little warmed cream to the pasta as you are tossing with the cheese.

penne with butternut squash
and toasted hickory nuts

Serves 2 as a main course or 4 as a side dish

1 medium butternut or other orange squash (about 4 cups of cubes)

3 tablespoons extra-virgin olive oil

3 tablespoons finely chopped red onion

1 small sweet red pepper, cut into ½-inch pieces (optional)

½ pound penne or garganelli pasta

4 to 5 medium fresh sage leaves, torn into small pieces

1 tablespoon butter

⅓ cup hickory nuts or pecans, toasted and coarsely chopped

½ cup Parmigiano-Reggiano cheese, freshly and finely grated, plus extra for the table

¼ cup cream, warmed (optional)

Salt and freshly ground pepper

Pinch or two of freshly grated nutmeg

Preheat oven to 400°F. Cut squash in half, scoop out seeds and stringy pulp, peel and cut into ½-inch cubes. Place on jelly-roll pan and toss with 1½ tablespoons of olive oil to coat lightly. Place in oven and roast 20 minutes or so, turning with a spatula occasionally. During the last 5 minutes of cooking, add onion and red pepper to the pan and toss with squash. Remove from oven when tender; be careful not to overcook.

While squash is roasting, boil pasta in salted water until al dente. Reserve 2 tablespoons of pasta water when draining. After squash is done and the oven is turned off, add the sage leaves and toss with squash. This can be done at the last minute just to heat the leaves and crisp them a bit while draining pasta.

Warm remaining olive oil and butter in a small saucepan until very lightly browned. Add nuts to the serving bowl, toss in pasta, cheese, squash, onion, red pepper, sage leaves, and warmed butter and oil. Stir in cream if you like or a couple of tablespoons of the reserved pasta water. Season to taste with salt, pepper and nutmeg. Serve immediately with extra cheese.

ingredient info

Look for garganelli (a quill-shaped, ridged pasta with a high egg content) at a store where high-quality dried pasta is sold.

al dente

Al dente in Italian literally means "to the tooth." In reference to cooking pasta, it means the desired texture—tender, but firm. Cooked pasta always should offer some resistance to the bite.

additions for the carnivore

Bits of lightly sautéed prosciutto, speck or other cured pork would be a fabulous addition if you're inclined toward extra protein.

I love all the sensations in this dish—the salty olives, spicy garlic, hot red pepper, earthy cauliflower, sharp cheese and sweet crunchy nuts. It's equally good with regular pasta, although I like to use whole-wheat when I can for that extra nutritional benefit. Also, I think the heartiness of the whole-wheat flour complements the complexity of flavors here. In a pinch, I've substituted capers when I didn't have enough olives.

spaghetti with roasted cauliflower and pecans

Serves 4 as a main course

1 cup pitted, brine-cured green or black olives (or combination)

1 cup fresh, flat-leaf parsley leaves (loosely packed)

1 medium head of cauliflower, cut into bite-sized florets

¼ cup extra-virgin olive oil

¾ pound whole-wheat spaghetti

4 large garlic cloves, minced

1 teaspoon (or more) dried red-pepper flakes

½ teaspoon salt

⅔ cup finely grated Pecorino Romano cheese, plus additional for the table

¾ cup pecans or hickory nuts (or combination), toasted and coarsely chopped

Preheat oven to 425°F. Coarsely chop olives and parsley, place in a large bowl and set aside. Rinse and drain cauliflower, then place on a rimmed baking sheet and drizzle with olive oil, tossing to coat. Roast cauliflower 10 to 12 minutes or until golden brown, stirring occasionally.

Meanwhile, cook pasta in a large pot of boiling water. Remove cauliflower from oven and stir into bowl with olives and parsley. Add garlic, red-pepper flakes and salt. Toss well.

When pasta is al dente, drain and reserve a few tablespoons of pasta water. Add pasta to cauliflower mixture and toss well. Add cheese and nuts and toss again. If pasta is dry, moisten with a bit of pasta water and a little olive oil, if desired.

"**Everything you see I owe to spaghetti.**"

—Sophia Loren

nutty math

One pound of unshelled nuts yields
2¼ cups pecan halves
2 cups chopped pecans
1¼ cups hickory nuts
¾ to 1 cup black walnuts

Nutty math courtesy of University of Missouri Extension, Missouri Department of Agriculture and Missouri Northern Pecan Growers.

Missouri's robust black walnut is the perfect complement to the zesty fresh ginger in this dipping cookie. When you dunk one in your morning coffee or tea, you'll be so happy you made them—and so will those with whom you share a few.

black-walnut chocolate biscotti

Makes about 3 dozen cookies

2½ cups flour

1 cup sugar

1 teaspoon baking soda

½ teaspoon salt

¼ teaspoon cinnamon

¼ teaspoon ground cloves

2 tablespoons unsweetened cocoa powder

2 tablespoons grated fresh ginger root (peeled)

½ teaspoon vanilla

3 eggs

1 cup black walnuts (toasted lightly; skins removed as much as possible and chopped coarsely)

¼ cup almonds, toasted lightly and coarsely chopped

removing walnut skins

While the nuts are still hot from toasting, wrap them in a tea towel and rub them lightly against each other to remove as much skin as possible. Then proceed with chopping.

This batter can be mixed in a large bowl by hand, but is much easier with a food processor or large electric mixer. Blend dry ingredients (flour through cocoa powder) until mixture is well combined. In a small bowl, whisk together the ginger root, vanilla and eggs; add to the dry ingredients, beating until a dough is formed. Stir nuts in by hand.

Preheat oven to 350°F. Turn dough out onto lightly floured surface and knead several times. Divide into thirds. Butter and flour baking sheet. With floured hands, form each piece of dough into a 10- by 2½-inch log. Flatten lightly with hands. Arrange logs on sheet 4 inches apart.

Bake for 25 minutes. Let cool on baking sheet on a rack for 10 minutes. Remove logs from sheet and cut each crosswise on the diagonal into ¾-inch-thick slices. Arrange biscotti, cut sides down, on two baking sheets and bake for 5 minutes on each side. Transfer biscotti to racks to cool. Store in airtight containers. Will keep for two weeks.

Optional glaze

I like to dress up my biscotti by zigzagging chocolate down the lengths or by dipping the ends in chocolate. Here's how: Melt 3 ounces of high-quality dark chocolate and 2 tablespoons unsalted butter together over low heat. Remove from heat and add 2 tablespoons corn syrup (and just a touch of your favorite liqueur, if desired). Stir well and fill a pastry bag fitted with a small, round tip.

After cookies are cooled, squeeze chocolate through the pastry bag's tip in thin ribbons down the length of the cookie. Alternatively, dip ends in the warm chocolate and shake gently to remove excess. Dry thoroughly on racks before storing.

Holiday sweets made with native Missouri nuts (pecans, hickories and black walnuts). In star basket, Black-Walnut Chocolate Biscotti; on the tray, Date and Nut Bars, Zimmerschied and Papassinos; in wooden bowl, Craig's Picante Pecans.

This recipe is from family friend Ilse Hochhalter of High Hill, who came across it at the Deutschheim State Historic Site in Hermann, where she once worked as a guide and translator. Its Missouri origins appear to be from Cole Camp, a town south of Sedalia. "I discovered on a visit to Cole Camp," said Ilse, "that the name 'Zimmerschied' appeared on a tombstone of a family grave site. So, evidently, the cookie was a favorite once upon a time in the Zimmerschied family." The recipe was brought from Lower Saxony in the 1840s and altered throughout the years to adapt to local ingredients.

Zimmerschied
(German brown sugar cookies)

Makes about 10 dozen cookies

1 cup butter

1 teaspoon vanilla

1 cup dark brown sugar, packed

2½ cups flour (I use a little less)

1 teaspoon baking soda

Pinch of salt

1 cup Missouri black walnuts, chopped

Preheat oven to 350°F. Cream butter, vanilla and sugar thoroughly. In another bowl, mix flour, soda and salt. Combine dry and wet ingredients, adding walnuts last. Shape into rolls, seal tightly and refrigerate overnight. Slice about ⅓-inch thick and bake on ungreased baking sheets 15 to 20 minutes or until bottoms are nicely browned.

a note about size and number

I made four rolls, which yielded small cookies—about an inch across. You could make fewer rolls and, consequently, larger cookies; however, they are very rich and the one-bite size seems perfect.

I make these chewy date bars for Christmas every year and serve them with the Dryden family's rich drinking custard. This recipe is adapted from *The New York Times Cook Book* by Craig Claiborne, one of my early cooking mentors.

date and nut bars
Makes 2 to 3 dozen bars

½ cup coarsely chopped black walnuts

½ cup coarsely chopped pecans

½ cup dates, pitted and chopped

¾ cup sifted flour, plus 1 tablespoon

3 eggs

1½ cups brown sugar, firmly packed

¾ teaspoon baking powder

¼ teaspoon salt

⅓ cup powdered sugar, sifted

A bit of butter for greasing pan

Preheat oven to 350°F. Butter a 9- by 12-inch pan, line it with parchment paper, and butter the paper.

In a small bowl, combine nuts and dates. Add 1 tablespoon flour and mix with fingers until dates are coated and mixed with nuts. Set aside.

In another bowl, beat eggs, add sugar gradually and continue beating until fluffy. Sift together remaining flour, baking powder and salt. Add to egg mixture and stir until well mixed. Stir dates and nuts into the batter.

Spread over parchment paper and bake for about 30 minutes or until cake rebounds to the touch when pressed gently in the center. Cool slightly, turn gently out of pan and cut the longer dimension into 1-inch-wide strips. Then cut each strip into thirds or fourths. Gently dab bars in powdered sugar while they are still warm.

I ate these little diamond-shaped gems throughout the Italian island of Sardinia. Traditionally made with English walnuts and almonds, they also adapt well to Missouri nuts. Here I've substituted pecans and hickory nuts for the walnuts. They're a perfect addition to your holiday cookie tray.

papassinos (Sardinian raisin-and-nut shortbread cookies)

Makes about 3 dozen cookies

Cookies

½ cup unsalted butter

¾ cup sugar

2 teaspoons grated orange or tangerine peel

2 eggs

2 tablespoons fresh orange or tangerine juice

1½ cups flour

¼ teaspoon salt

⅔ cup golden raisins

⅔ cup toasted almonds, coarsely chopped

⅔ cup pecans and/or hickory nuts, coarsely chopped

Glaze

⅓ cup powdered sugar, sifted

1 tablespoon fresh orange or tangerine juice

Prepare cookies

Cream butter, sugar and citrus peel in food processor or electric mixer. Beat in eggs one at a time; then beat in juice. Add flour and salt, and mix well. Stir in raisins and nuts. Wrap dough in plastic (it will be very moist) and refrigerate at least four hours.

Preheat oven to 350°F. Roll out dough on floured surface to about ⅜-inch thick. With a floured knife, cut into diamonds (cut 1½-inch-wide strips first, and then crisscross strips in diagonal cuts spaced 1½ inches apart). Arrange on ungreased baking sheets, spacing 1 inch apart. Bake until golden, about 20 minutes. Transfer to racks.

Prepare glaze

Mix powdered sugar with juice. Brush glaze over warm cookies. Cool and store cookies in airtight containers.

From top are Date and Nut Bars, Zimmerschied *and* Papassinos.

R ich and creamy, this ice cream may be my favorite way to savor Missouri's black walnuts. See page 148 for more details about making gelato.

black-walnut gelato
with lacy spice wafers

1½ cups black walnuts
2 cups milk
3 egg yolks
3 tablespoons sugar
4 tablespoons maple syrup

> "I doubt the world holds for anyone a more soul-stirring surprise than the first adventure with ice cream."
>
> —Heywood Broun

Equipment: cheesecloth and home ice-cream freezer

Toast walnuts until lightly browned, turning frequently. While the nuts are still hot from toasting, wrap them in a tea towel and rub them lightly against each other to remove as much skin as possible. Grind them in a blender until they are a fine paste. Heat the milk in a saucepan over medium heat until the edge is ringed with tiny bubbles. Turn the heat off immediately and add the nut paste. Mix thoroughly and cover the pan. Allow to cool completely.

Line a strainer with a double thickness of cheesecloth and set over a bowl. Pour the nut-and-milk mixture into the strainer and, with a wooden spoon, press as much of it as possible into the bowl. Since it is thick, only a small amount will go through. Keep pressing until you have expressed as much of the liquid as you can. At that point, squeeze the cheesecloth gently with your hands, forcing through as much as possible.

In another bowl, beat the egg yolks and sugar until the yolks are pale and foamy. Add the strained nut-and-milk mixture to the eggs, mixing it in a little at a time, along with the maple syrup.

Pour into the top part of a double boiler and turn on the heat to medium. Stir constantly and cook for 3 to 4 minutes after the water in the lower half of the pot has begun to bubble.

Pour mixture into a bowl and allow to cool completely. When cool, chill in the refrigerator for at least 1 hour. Place the mixture in the ice-cream maker and follow the manufacturer's instructions. When done, allow the ice cream to firm up for 30 to 45 minutes in the freezer before serving. If prepared a day or two in advance, take it out of your freezer and place in the refrigerator for 30 minutes before serving, so it will soften to a creamy consistency.

Serve with *Lacy Spice Wafers*. (They're optional, but delightful.)

lacy spice wafers

10 to 12 large wafers or 20 small ones

4 tablespoons unsalted butter
¼ cup packed light brown sugar
3 tablespoons honey
¼ cup flour
½ teaspoon freshly ground cloves
½ teaspoon freshly grated nutmeg
½ teaspoon cinnamon
Pinch of cocoa powder
Pinch of salt

Preheat oven to 375°F. In a small saucepan, melt butter with brown sugar and honey over moderate heat. Stir occasionally until the sugar is dissolved. Remove pan from the heat and stir in the flour, spices, cocoa powder and salt. Mix well. Drop rounded teaspoons of batter 3 inches apart onto ungreased baking sheet. Bake 6 minutes or until golden.

Let cool for a minute before trying to remove wafers from the sheet. Remove one wafer with a thin metal spatula and immediately drape over a rolling pin to create a curved shape. Cool completely on the rolling pin; make remainder of the wafers in the same manner. Transfer to airtight containers. They will keep several days in a container at room temperature. Scoop ice cream into serving dishes and insert one or two wafers at an angle into each scoop.

ice cream in a wafer basket

Here's another method that makes a pretty presentation. Instead of curving warm wafers around a rolling pin, carefully and very quickly press each wafer into a glass sherbet dish to mold the wafer to the dish's shape. Some find it easier to place the wafers over upturned drinking glasses and gently mold them around the bottoms of the glasses. Either way, each will make a delicate "basket" to later hold the ice cream. This should be done no more than a few hours before serving.

This amount sounds like a lot, but once you have the oven going, you may as well take advantage of two shelves. Besides, you'll go through it quickly. It's great as morning cereal with milk or yogurt, and very tasty as a dry snack. Sprinkle a little on your oatmeal for a welcome crunch.

pecan-orange granola

Makes about 5 pounds (a generous gallon) of granola

8 cups rolled oats

2 cups coarsely chopped pecans

2 cups raw sunflower seeds

1 cup sesame seeds

1 cup shredded unsweetened coconut

1 teaspoon salt

1 cup honey

¾ cup vegetable oil

1 teaspoon almond extract

Juice and zest (chopped) of 4 oranges

2 cups chopped dried fruit

Preheat oven to 350°F. In a large mixing bowl, toss together the oats, nuts, seeds, coconut and salt. Over low heat, warm the honey and oil in a medium saucepan, stirring until well combined. Remove from heat and stir in almond extract and orange juice. Pour over the dry ingredients and stir well with a wooden spoon. Work the mixture with your hands, if needed, until everything is damp.

Spread mixture no deeper than ½ inch on large, rimmed baking sheets. Bake for 30 to 40 minutes, stirring several times, until crispy and golden. When the granola has cooled, stir in the zest and dried fruit. Store granola in jars.

a good shelf cleaner (and infinitely variable)

Granola is a good place to use up dabs of grains, seeds and dried fruit that may be languishing on your shelves. I make different substitutions each time I make this. Consider using part rolled wheat or barley instead of all oats; part maple syrup instead of all honey; part pumpkin, poppy or flax seeds instead of all sesame; and any combination of dried cranberries, mangoes, cherries, figs, raisins, currants and dates.

Friend and fine cook, Bonnie Chasteen, says she developed this recipe after being disappointed by other sweet-potato biscuit recipes she'd run across. "These are tender on the inside," Bonnie says, "and crunchy on the outside. Try making them with as many locally produced and native ingredients as you can find—flours, honeys, nuts, sweet potatoes, butter and buttermilk. Whip them up at Thanksgiving, and your family and friends will be extra grateful!"

Bonnie's sweet potato-pecan drop biscuits

Makes 12 cat-head-sized biscuits or 30 walnut-sized ones

2 cups flour

1 tablespoon baking powder

½ teaspoon baking soda

1 teaspoon salt

Whole nutmeg

6 tablespoons butter, finely cut

⅓ cup pecans or black walnuts, toasted and chopped

1 large sweet potato (12 to 14 ounces), cooked, peeled and mashed; canned sweet potatoes or pumpkin may be substituted

1 generous cup buttermilk

1 tablespoon honey

Preheat oven to 425°F and grease a big cookie sheet. Sift together the first four ingredients (through salt) and a few light gratings of nutmeg. Rub butter into the mixture until it feels like cornmeal—lumps are normal. Stir in nuts.

Mix together sweet potato, buttermilk and honey; gently add to other ingredients until just combined. (If batter seems too dry, pour in a little more buttermilk—go slowly—until all the flour is incorporated. Don't over-wet or over-mix—it's good if the dough is rough and lumpy. If you put in too much liquid or stir too long, the biscuits will turn out flabby and soggy.)

With two big spoons, scoop and scrape biscuits onto the greased cookie sheet. If you want to go to the trouble of rolling and cutting them on a floured surface, help yourself. The dough holds up just fine. Bake for 15 minutes or until you can smell them and the tops are lightly browned.

ingredient tip

Any mix of white, whole-wheat, oat, spelt or rye flour works here. A little oat bran or ground flax seeds don't hurt, either.

butter and ham them up

These are lovely at breakfast with any kind of fruit butter—peach, apple, pear or pumpkin. When sliced and stuffed with a bit of country ham and mustard, the smaller-sized biscuits will receive raves as appetizers. Serve them at your next brunch buffet.

I inherited an old Kieffer pear tree with my house, and almost every year in late October it drops a bounty of fruit in my yard. Squirrels and raccoons occasionally take bites out of the pears and leave the rest for me. I cook them up in all kinds of things. Though coarse in texture, the pears have a delicious, winey taste and make good sauce, baked goodies and chutneys. They are a nice companion to the pecans in this little cake.

upside-down pear-pecan gingerbread

Serves 8 to 10

Topping

½ cup sugar

2 tablespoons water

2 tablespoons butter

2 cups chopped pears (1-inch chunks)

24 pecan halves

Cake

1 cup white flour

½ cup whole-wheat flour

1 teaspoon baking soda

1 teaspoon ground ginger

½ teaspoon freshly grated ginger root (peeled)

½ teaspoon cinnamon

¼ teaspoon nutmeg

¼ teaspoon allspice

¼ teaspoon salt

⅓ cup butter

½ cup sugar

1 egg

¼ cup honey

½ cup buttermilk

Preheat oven to 350°F. Combine first three topping ingredients in a small saucepan; heat on low and stir until butter melts. Blend all well and pour into baking dish. Spoon pears evenly over the mixture, and press pecan halves gently into the pears, arranging so there are three halves per serving.

Stir together the next nine ingredients (through salt) in a bowl and set aside. In another bowl, beat together the butter and sugar until light and fluffy. Add egg and beat well. Combine honey and buttermilk. Stir into the creamed mixture, alternating with the dry ingredients.

Pour batter over pears in the dish. Bake 30 to 35 minutes, or until a toothpick inserted in the middle comes out clean. Cool for a few minutes before running a knife around the edges of the cake and turning onto a serving plate. Serve warm or at room temperature with a bit of freshly whipped cream or scoop of ginger or vanilla ice cream. Good with either coffee or rooibos tea.

cooking with the seasons

This recipe is adapted from *Simply in Season*. A cookbook by Mary Beth Lind and Cathleen Hockman-Wert, it offers good recipes and equally good reasons to eat seasonal foods grown locally.

These are among the lightest and most delicious pancakes I've ever tasted—and I've tasted and made quite a few. Native pecans and apples are the crowning touch on the tender, maple-syrup-drenched cakes. The recipe is adapted from one in *Bon Appétit* magazine.

pancakes
with Missouri maple syrup, apples and pecans

Makes 12 medium pancakes

Maple-syrup apples

2 tablespoons unsalted butter

3 large Missouri apples (peeled, cored and cut into ½-inch-thick slices)

½ cup (or slightly more) maple syrup

½ teaspoon cinnamon

Pancakes

⅔ cup white flour

⅓ cup whole-wheat flour

2 tablespoons yellow cornmeal

2 tablespoons turbinado or brown sugar

1 teaspoon baking powder

1 teaspoon baking soda

½ teaspoon salt

1 cup buttermilk

1 cup plain low-fat yogurt

1 large egg

1½ tablespoons unsalted butter, melted

24 Missouri pecan halves, lightly toasted

Additional unsalted butter for the griddle

Additional maple syrup

For maple-syrup apples

Melt butter in a large skillet over medium-high heat. Add apples and 1 tablespoon maple syrup. Sauté for a few minutes until apples are tender. Mix in remaining maple syrup and cinnamon. Turn off heat and reheat briefly, if desired, just before the last pancake is cooked.

For pancakes

Whisk together dry ingredients in a large bowl. In another bowl, whisk buttermilk, yogurt and egg together until well blended. Add to dry ingredients and stir gently until just blended, but still lumpy (take care not to overmix). Gently mix in 1½ tablespoons melted butter.

Heat griddle over medium heat. Melt a thin coating of butter over griddle. Drop batter by ⅓ cupfuls onto griddle. Cook pancakes until brown on bottom and bubbles form on top. Flip cakes over and cook until bottoms are brown and pancakes are barely firm to the touch. Transfer to plates. Repeat with remaining batter, adding more butter to the griddle as needed. Spoon apples over pancakes and sprinkle with nuts. Set additional maple syrup at the table.

make your own maple syrup

Fragrant and delicious, maple syrup is an original American treat. Learn how to make your own at Rockwoods Reservation's Maple Sugar Festival, held annually in February in St. Louis County.

Bring your family and discover how Native Americans and early settlers tapped maple trees, collected sap and boiled it down to make syrup. Walk through the woods and learn how to identify maple trees after their leaves have dropped. Collect your own sap, boil your own syrup—and enjoy the sweet taste of success.

There's no charge for the festival and no reservations are required. However, if your school or group (25 to 35 people) can't attend the festival and wants to enjoy the Maple Sugar program, please call 636-458-2236 to make a reservation. Rockwoods Reservation is located at 2751 Glencoe Road in Wildwood.

holiday bow ties
with sun-dried tomatoes and toasted pecans

1 cup boiling water
1 cup sun-dried tomatoes
4 large garlic cloves
¾ cup finely grated Parmigiano-Reggiano cheese
¾ cup finely grated Pecorino Romano cheese
6 tablespoons finely chopped pecans, lightly toasted
⅔ cup extra-virgin olive oil
½ teaspoon salt
1½ pounds farfalle (bow tie) pasta

Pour water over tomatoes in medium bowl and let sit 20 minutes or until plump, stirring occasionally. Drain. (It's okay if there is a slight amount of liquid left.) Chop garlic finely in food processor. Add drained tomatoes to processor and chop until fine. Remove and put in bowl with cheeses, pecans, oil and salt. Mix well.

Bring 6 quarts of water and a pinch of salt to a boil in a large pot. Cook pasta until tender to the bite. Drain, reserving a tablespoon of the pasta water with the pasta. Toss immediately with the sauce ingredients in the bowl. Mix well. Serve in a large bowl, with extra cheese on the table.

"The pleasures of the table are for every man, of every land, and no matter of what place in history or society; they can be a part of all his other pleasures, and they last the longest, to console him when he has outlived the rest."

—Jean-Anthelme Brillat-Savarin

festive, fast and fantastic

This is a festive pasta and sauce that is perfect for busy cooks. Quick to assemble, the sauce can be made in advance and will keep, refrigerated, for a week. If you want to serve fewer people than mentioned above, simply use ½ cup of sauce to ½ pound of pasta for 2 main dishes or 4 side dishes; 1 cup of sauce to 1 pound of pasta for 4 main dishes or 8 side dishes. The sauce is equally good with linguine, spaghetti or medium shells.

Spicy pecans were among the treats at a Slow Food Katy Trail tapas party hosted by The Wine Cellar & Bistro in Columbia one summer evening. I loved the herby-floral-spicy taste that Chef Craig Cyr created with this combination. He detailed his list of ingredients for me, and months later I came up with the proportions that I thought would do justice to my memory. Feel free to adjust quantities to your taste, depending upon the balance of salty, spicy and sweet that you prefer.

Craig's picante pecans

Makes 1 cup of spicy pecans

3 tablespoons unsalted butter
1½ teaspoons fennel seeds, slightly crushed
1½ teaspoons fresh rosemary, coarsely chopped
1½ teaspoons lavender buds, coarsely chopped
1½ teaspoons red pepper, crushed
Several pinches coarse sea salt, slightly crushed
Several twists of black pepper from the pepper mill
2 tablespoons Missouri maple syrup
1 cup Missouri pecans

Preheat oven to 350°F. Melt butter in a small saucepan.

Add fennel seeds and lightly toast, stirring. Add herbs and stir for a moment until they begin to release some of their oils. Add remaining ingredients and toss well.

Pour mixture onto a rimmed baking sheet and bake until toasted, about 5 to 8 minutes (depending upon the size of the nut). Stir several times during baking to make sure the pecans are well coated and that their grooves are stuffed with herby, spicy bits. Watch carefully to make sure they don't get too brown.

Remove from oven and spread out on a cool baking sheet. When cooled, store in an airtight container.

nutty ideas

These are great with a nice Spanish sparkler on your party table. They also add a crunchy zip to fresh salad greens that have been tossed with a lemony vinaigrette. The toasty little clumps of spicy, herby butter are tasty, too.

Fruits

fruits
tantalizing treats begging to be picked

I've always been a gatherer, with a lifelong affinity for picking just about anything edible. As a child in High Hill, I would walk along the railroad tracks in search of wild strawberries, and while away an early-summer morning in a neighbor's backyard gooseberry patch. Some of my fondest childhood food memories find me stooping next to my mother as we gathered dandelion, lamb's quarters, poke and dock in the field behind our house for one of my favorite spring meals—wild greens cooked with fresh hog jowl and topped with cornmeal dumplings.

This picking passion follows me wherever I am. In foreign lands, I often pick interesting-looking fruits or nuts when hiking in the countryside, and sample them if I'm feeling brave (or have seen them in nearby outdoor markets or their pictures on liqueur bottles). My idea of summer fun when I lived in Oregon was to spend the weekend in the Willamette Valley's bountiful blueberry, strawberry and caneberry fields. In the fall I could be found on ladders in the pear and apple orchards, and was ecstatic one year when an acquaintance gave me carte blanche on his prune-plum ranch. I spent the next week drying plums by the bucketsful.

When I returned to my Missouri roots and began working at the Conservation Department, my appreciation for the state's native fruits began to deepen. Each summer I wade among the gooseberry thorns again, as I did as a child, and stain my hands with blackberries—eating one for every two I pick. Lately, I've also learned about the culinary joys of late-summer elderberries. In the fall, I look forward to outsmarting a few deer and possums for a chance to fill my baskets with pawpaws and persimmons.

Bonnie Chasteen and Byron Smith sort through persimmons they gathered on a mid-Missouri November afternoon. Bonnie, who was reared in North Carolina, says she grew up surrounded by persimmons, but failed to appreciate them because of an unfortunate early experience. "I tasted an unripe one as a child, and as a result, I refused to try them again until decades later—after moving to Missouri. I couldn't believe how wonderful and sweet they were and how I had been missing out on them for years just because of that one incident!"

Smith remembers loving them as a child on his grandparents' farm in Boone County. "My grandmother would make jams from them, and I remember how good those were and how I also loved eating them fresh from the trees." As a Missouri landscape painter, Smith is taken with the persimmon's vibrant orange color and form.

144

the persimmon—a tree of many charms and myths

I am amazed by the number of times I've offered a freshly picked persimmon to friends or neighbors, only to be quickly turned down. With a little prodding, I discover they've never tried one, but have been warned about how their mouths will pucker if they dare. This will happen only when the fruit is unripe, however. Having tasted a few of those (usually once a season—just to test how ripeness is progressing in certain trees), I can say that it is a fleeting discomfort. Like other unpleasant life experiences, once you do it a few times you develop better judgment as a result. Never would I consider forfeiting the pure bliss of eating ripe persimmons just because of a little temporary tartness!

Another notion that needs adjustment is that one must wait until after a hard frost to eat the fruit. Every year I graze on different trees in various locations from September to November—before and after a frost. Ripe fruits will yield to slight pressure when you squeeze them, but taste tests at different times are essential; they're the only way you'll learn when a particular tree is ready.

Not only are the globe-shaped fruits delicious, but beautiful to look at when hanging from the tree. However, when smashed through a food mill, I think they are at their most beautiful; the orange color of the resulting pulp is unsurpassed in nature's palette, and it thrills me anew each time I see it!

blackberries

No other fruit says summer in Missouri like blackberries—dangling in the scorching heat from their arching canes like big black jewels, their sweet taste is so alluring we'll brave chiggers and a few thorny scratches. A favorite for jams, pies and other desserts, the berries also add a sparkle to salads and other savory dishes, as well. Common throughout the state, blackberry brambles provide food and cover for many birds and small mammals. Deer and turkeys also eat the fruit. The abundance of rains in late spring to early summer determines the fruit size and quality.

gooseberries

In addition to providing delicious fruit for dishes sweet and savory, the gooseberry shrub furnishes excellent cover for small mammals and birds—some of which eat the berries. With leaves as pretty as its fruit, it also makes a nice landscaping plant. Consider adding a few of these attractive members of the currant family to your vegetable or bird garden, or along the edge of your woodland.

pawpaws

The pawpaw tree has the distinction of producing the country's largest native fruit. This member of a family of tropical fruits evolved to tolerate cold temperatures and is found growing wild in the forests of about 30 states and Ontario. Its fruit grows in clusters along the tree's branches and ripens in Missouri in August and September. Resembling a smooth, greenish-yellow potato, it has sweet and flavorful, custard-like flesh.

The tree grows in dense shade, tucked away in groves or "patches" in moist, cool hollows, in river bottoms and on fertile, wooded slopes beside streams. Wildlife, including opossums, raccoons, quail, turkeys and many birds, relish the fruit. To beat the animals to

it, some people pick the fruit while it's still on the tree. When I worked at the Conservation Department building in Jefferson City, I often would follow the ripening progression of the fruits hanging on a tree not far from my office. More often than not, something or somebody would beat me to them.

Picking up pawpaws was a much revered fall activity for many early settlers in Missouri, but today it seems that most of the fruits are left for the animals to enjoy. In recent years, however, the pawpaw has attracted the interest of horticulturists, landscapers, commercial fruit growers and researchers. One Saturday last fall, the University of Missouri's Center for Agroforestry featured a pawpaw tasting at Columbia Farmers Market. A plentiful crop of cultivated pawpaws at the Horticulture and Agroforestry Research Center (HARC) in New Franklin allowed the fruit to be showcased. First-time pawpaw tasters seemed to be delighted and surprised that there was such a tropical-tasting fruit growing in Missouri's woods.

Michael Gold, an MU professor and associate director of HARC, said this effort to market the pawpaw in Mid-Missouri is part of the research center's goal to help family farms find alternative enterprises. "We're further along in our efforts with black walnuts," Gold said of encouraging Missourians to grow the native trees for economic opportunities. However, he hopes that Missouri farmers also will take an interest in growing cultivated varieties of pawpaws (which, according to Gold, achieve much higher yields and fruit sizes when grown in full sunlight).

elderberries—a fruit with a fan club

Elderberry shrubs can be found everywhere in Missouri—in open woods, thickets, along streams, fencerows, roadsides and railroads. The plant is an important food source for several mammals and more than 40 species of birds.

It's popular with humans, too. Missouri foragers gather its flowers and fruits to make wines, syrups, muffins and many other edibles. Europeans have appreciated it for centuries, both in the wild and cultivated. It is estimated that more than 1,000 farmers in Austria, alone, grow elderberries.

Its cultivation has been gaining more and more admirers throughout the United States, too, due in large part to one of its biggest fans: Terry Durham, owner of Eridu Farms near Hartsburg. A lifelong elderberry enthusiast, Durham has planted 20 acres of his farm to the shrub and is planning for more. He uses no sprays on the plants; instead, he interplants other native species among the berries in an effort to create a sustainable, diverse agriculture of native plants.

I attended the fifth annual elderberry conference at his farm in 2010, which drew 100 growers and would-be growers from 13 states and Canada. Funded by a grant from the Missouri Department of Agriculture, two days of workshops introduced small-farm producers to the potential of elderberry-juice production.

Durham (left) says that one native variety from the Osage River area can produce 12,000 pounds of fruit per acre. However, he notes that it takes two pounds of berries to make 11 ounces of juice. In addition to juice, Durham likes the fruits for making vinegars and ketchups. "The fruit has natural tenderizing qualities," he says, "which makes it a great marinade for meat." He also uses the flowers (right) to create a tasty cordial.

146

DAVID BRUNS

147

blackberry gelato

Serves 6

1 pound blackberries (about 2 cups)
¾ to 1 cup sugar
½ cup water
½ cup heavy cream or plain yogurt
   (I use low-fat, but whole-milk works also)

Mix blackberries and sugar in food processor until thoroughly blended. Then add water and blend well again. Taste for sweetness. Press mixture through a fine-mesh strainer into a metal bowl, leaving solids in strainer. Set aside.

If using cream, whip it in another bowl until it thickens slightly (to the consistency of buttermilk). Whisk cream or yogurt gently into the fruit mixture, combining thoroughly. Taste (of course); the fresh-fruit flavor should shine through. Add more sugar if you find it not sweet enough (however, it's best to add sugar while mixture is still in the food processor and can be spun around again). If you like it now, you'll love it after it's frozen. Cover bowl and chill for at least 1 hour. I often leave it overnight in the refrigerator.

Pour into container of your ice-cream maker and freeze, following the manufacturer's instructions. This makes about 3 cups of gorgeously purple-red gelato. Dip it up into your prettiest dessert dishes and top with pieces of the fruit.

measurement confession

Although I follow the base recipe above for all fruit gelato, I vary the sugar, water and yogurt (or cream) quantities based upon the sweetness and density of the fruit. So, tasting along the way and experimentation is necessary; make it to suit your own taste. Of course, using the sweetest, freshest and juiciest fruit always yields the best results.

gelato—a love story

I believe that the Italian way of making ice cream is the purest and freshest expression of a frozen-fruit dessert. The gelato-maker's art encompasses flavors other than fruit, of course, but it is with fruit where I've always felt their (and, most assuredly, my) passion lies. With the fresh-fruit essence always front and center, the flavor is never too sweet or rich. However, the texture is reliably creamy and smooth.

I've always been dazzled by the variety of gelato flavors throughout Italy. In cities with several competing shops, each attempts to outdo the other with fantastic ranges of flavors and displays. It's a rare passerby who doesn't succumb to the constant allure of mounds of gorgeous colors, artfully arranged fresh fruit and arching 3-foot stacks of cones. In addition to blood orange, fig, pear, prune, kiwi and tangerine, I've swooned over flavors such as jasmine, pine nut, chestnut, balsamic vinegar, rice and tiramisu.

I learned to make gelato 30 years ago in Marcella Hazan's cooking class in Bologna, and I've never stopped experimenting with flavors. Of course, native Missouri black walnuts, blackberries, persimmons, pawpaws—and even gooseberries—all make delightful ice cream, and I've included their recipes in this book. While Italian gelato-making tradition calls for using a bit of heavy cream, I've substituted yogurt with just-as-delicious results. Try your hand with blackberry first and see if you can ever go back to eating fruit ice cream any other way. Recipes are adapted from Marcella Hazan's *The Classic Italian Cook Book*.

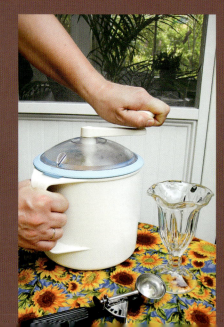

the ever-ready ice-cream maker

I use a Donvier ice-cream maker, whose canister I keep in the freezer at all times—ready to pull out when I have the frequent summer urge to make fresh-fruit gelato or frozen yogurt.

additional freezing
for firmer texture

Freshly made gelato will be rather soft, but
ready to eat. If you like it a little more firm,
spoon it into a plastic container with a tight-
sealing lid and put it in the freezer for several
hours. Letting it soften slightly after removal
from the freezer will make the dipping easier.

149

Nothing evokes summer childhood memories as much for me as my mother's blackberry cobbler—bubbling and oozing its purple-red juices through the fork pricks on the top crust. I also remember the heat of the kitchen on those 100-degree days. This lovely dessert eliminates that problem, making use of summer's plentiful and delicious black jewels without the necessity of turning on the oven. You may use all blackberries if you like, or part raspberries, as well. The types of berries and their ratios are flexible. If you have a pudding basin, pull it out for use in this pudding of British origin. Otherwise, a glass bowl works well because it allows you to see patches of bread that need to absorb juice. Another bonus is that this can be made a day or two in advance, and is just as delicious.

summer black-and-blue pudding

Serves 8 to 10

1-pound rectangular or long loaf of good-quality, firm-textured white bread such as a batard, crusts discarded

5 cups blackberries

4 cups blueberries

1 cup sugar

1 teaspoon fresh lemon juice

"The stove, the bins, the cupboards, I had learned forever, make an inviolable throne room. From them I ruled; temporarily I controlled. I felt powerful, and I loved that feeling."

—M.F.K. Fisher

Cut loaf into ½-inch-thick slices. Cut out a 3- or 4-inch round from 1 slice and fit snugly into the bottom of a 2½-quart bowl. (Preferably, the bowl should be 8 inches in diameter across the top and 3 or 4 inches across the bottom. The shape of the bowl supports the bread slices stacked atop one another.) Line the inside of the bowl with 10 to 12 slices, overlapping them slightly.

Bring berries, sugar and lemon juice to a boil in a medium saucepan over medium heat. Reduce heat to simmer and stir occasionally until berries soften and release their juices, 8 to 10 minutes. Spoon fruit into a fine mesh strainer set over a bowl and let drain 15 minutes. Spoon a bit of the reserved juices onto the bread in the bottom of the bowl—enough to fully color the bread. Spoon drained fruit into bread-lined bowl, reserving juices for later use. Cover completely with remaining bread, cutting bread to fit. Pour juices evenly over bread, making sure all bread is saturated.

Cover pudding directly with a piece of wax paper, and place a flat dish or plate to fit against the pudding. Don't worry if the pudding is not flush with the top of the bowl. The important thing is for the plate to fit snugly against the pudding; therefore, if necessary, use one to fit inside the bowl. Put a 2- or 3-pound weight (a large can or whatever is handy and won't hurt to be refrigerated) on the plate and chill at least 8 hours.

Remove weight, plate and wax paper. Carefully run a dull knife around the inside to loosen (if necessary) and invert cake stand or other decorative dish over bowl. Turn upside down and carefully unmold. Decorate plate with extra berries, and serve with whipped sweetened cream if you desire.

Years ago I ran across this interesting way of making a delicious uncooked blackberry spread that is wonderful on toast and hot rolls or over vanilla ice cream. I also use it with peanut butter to make a quick sandwich. I believe it is a method passed on by the late Edna Lewis, who was a fine Southern chef and author. The beauty of it lies in its simplicity. It requires only minutes to make and will keep for many months when refrigerated.

no-cook blackberry spread

Makes about 3 cups of spread

3 cups blackberries
3 cups sugar
½ teaspoon salt

Combine all ingredients in a bowl and mash with a potato masher until berries are liquefied and sugar has dissolved. Cover and chill the spread for 3 days, allowing flavors to develop. Stir once a day. Pour into jars and keep in the refrigerator.

keep this one chilled

This spread must be kept in the refrigerator; it is not intended for sitting on a pantry shelf.

If you've made enough blackberry jam and pies for the summer, but still have extra berries on hand, put them to use in this delightful after-dinner drink. It takes just a few minutes to make and requires no heat—just some steeping time and a weekly stir. Should you want to increase the quantities suggested below, bump up the size of the steeping jar accordingly.

blackberry cordial

Makes 1½ cups of liqueur

½ cup sugar
1 cup blackberries, gently rinsed
1 cup vodka

Put sugar in a 1-quart glass jar with a lid. Add berries and vodka, and cover with lid. Put in a cool, dark place. Every week for 2 months, open the jar and stir mixture. For fullest flavor, however, let the mixture steep another couple of months. So, if you start the process during peak Missouri blackberry season, you easily will have a delicious and beautiful cordial to drink or give as a gift at Thanksgiving or Christmas. Strain the finished cordial through a fine sieve, and pour into the serving bottle of your choice.

Blackberry cordials and Martha Folk's chocolate-pistachio biscotti bring a holiday dinner to a perfect end.

Beautiful little purple-black elderberries lend a slightly crunchy texture, subtle flavor and eye-catching color to these lightly sweet corn muffins.

elderberry-lemon corn muffins

¾ cup flour

½ cup sugar

4 teaspoons baking powder

1 teaspoon salt

1¼ cups coarsely ground yellow cornmeal

2 eggs

1 cup milk

¼ cup vegetable oil

1 teaspoon lemon juice

Zest of 1 medium lemon

1 cup elderberries

Preheat oven to 425°F and line a 12-muffin tin with paper baking cups.

Sift flour with sugar, baking powder and salt in a medium bowl; stir in cornmeal and blend well. Combine eggs, milk, oil, lemon juice and zest in another bowl and whisk until well blended. Add wet ingredients to dry and blend gently with a spatula until just combined; do not overbeat. Gently fold in elderberries and pour mixture into muffin tin.

Bake for approximately 15 minutes or until a toothpick stuck in the center of a muffin comes out clean.

blossoms on bicycles

Elderberries have enjoyed popularity in Europe for centuries and are used there for making wine, jellies, syrups, sauces, soups, tarts and food coloring. Restaurant menus in the Alps often feature the plant's flowers in sorbets, fritters, frittate and drinks.

According to one French elderflower-liqueur maker, the process of gathering the delicate blossoms for the distilling process is a carefully orchestrated sequence of events that must be completed during the short three- to four-day span when the blossoms peak. Alpine farmers allegedly handpick the elderflowers and transport them via bicycle to depots or private homes equipped with scales and special crates, where the flowers are meticulously guarded before arriving at the distillery.

155

If you have access to elderberry juice (homemade or commercially bottled), here are a couple of delicious ways to use it. Some people swear that a daily nip of the juice keeps them healthy.

quick and delicious elderberry drinks

elderberry lemonade

With a quick stir, a teaspoon of elderberry juice will turn a glass of plain lemonade into a beautiful color and a refreshing summer drink.

elderberry-vodka lemonade splash

Run water over a martini glass and chill it in the freezer just until a light skiff of ice forms. Pour into the glass ½ jigger of vodka, a teaspoon of elderberry juice and a couple of shots of lemonade. Add a twist or slice of lemon. This makes a hot August day almost bearable!

I'm enamored of the gorgeous color of elderberry syrup and its versatility. Add a few drops to a glass of sparkling water over ice, stir it into yogurt or drizzle some over vanilla ice cream, peach halves, pancakes and French toast. Pour a teaspoon or two in a flute or wine glass and top it off with your favorite sparkling or still white wine.

elderberry syrup

Makes 1 cup of syrup

¾ pound elderberries (2 packed cups)
1½ cups water
1 cup sugar
1 teaspoon fresh lemon juice

Put the elderberries in a large, non-reactive pot with the water. Bring to a boil, then reduce heat to a low boil and cook for 15 to 20 minutes, until berries are soft. Press through a fine sieve using a large spoon and discard the skins.

Pour the juice back into the pot, add sugar, and cook at a low boil over moderate heat for 15 minutes, until the syrup has thickened. It will thicken even more after it cools, so amount yielded depends somewhat upon how long it is cooked. Add lemon juice and cool completely. Pour into a jar and store in the refrigerator. It keeps for several months.

slick trick for removing stems

After you've plucked your elderberry clusters, you must remove the many woody stems before cooking. A nifty trick that Terry Durham of Eridu Farms taught me makes a laborious job a lot less so: Hold the berry clusters over a bowl and rake through them with a salad server (large three- or four-pronged fork). The berries will detach and fall into the bowl. You still may have to remove a few of the tiny stems—depending upon the delicacy of your recipe—but the hard work will be done! Another Missouri picker says she separates the berries from the stems by freezing them in resealable bags. While they are frozen, the tiny berries just pop off.

The pawpaw has a sweet, custard-like flesh. Some people say it tastes like a combination of banana, pineapple and mango. In any case, it makes for a tasty frozen dessert. See page 148 for more details about making gelato.

pawpaw frozen-yogurt gelato

Serves 4

5 pawpaws
⅓ cup sugar
¼ cup water
⅓ cup plain yogurt

Cut pawpaws in half and gently remove the pulp and seeds, emptying them into a food mill (be careful not to scrape the inside of the fruit's skin or the more fibrous pulp that is attached to the skin; both are bitter).

Force pulp through mill into a small bowl.

Whisk pulp and sugar together in a metal bowl until thoroughly blended. Then add water and blend well again. Whisk yogurt gently into the fruit mixture, combining thoroughly. Taste; the fresh-fruit flavor should shine through. Add more sugar if you find the mixture isn't sweet enough. Cover bowl and chill for at least 1 hour. I often leave it overnight in the refrigerator.

Pour into the container of your ice-cream maker and freeze, following the manufacturer's instructions.

if you're feeling skinny

I often use heavy cream instead of yogurt when I'm not feeling concerned about cutting calories. If using cream, whip it separately until it thickens a little, but not to the density of whipped cream. Then add it to the well-combined fruit, sugar and water mixture, and whisk gently until just blended.

159

Persimmons and pawpaws, being among the most perishable of fruits, beg for urgent attention once you have them in hand. One mid-September morning I concocted this coffee cake to make use of a gift of pawpaws from a friend's tree, persimmons I had picked up on a walk around the neighborhood, pears dropped in my yard from my old Kieffer pear tree and some southern Missouri pecans that were sitting on my counter. The cake has some wonderful attributes: it is quite moist, not too sweet, keeps several days and freezes well. In addition, the recipe is quite malleable; you may use the fruit in various proportions, leave out one or substitute another. It is based upon an Italian country recipe that uses pears, apples and bananas.

four-p coffee cake
with persimmons, pawpaws, pears and pecans

Serves 12

3 eggs

1⅓ cups sugar

⅛ teaspoon salt

2 tablespoons extra-virgin olive oil

Zest of 2 oranges

1 cup persimmon pulp (from about 3 dozen
   or 1½ pounds persimmons)

1 cup pawpaw pulp (from 2 medium pawpaws)

2 cups coarsely chopped pears (about 2 medium)

2 tablespoons fresh lemon juice

2¾ cups flour

2½ teaspoons baking powder

½ cup coarsely chopped pecans,
   plus 8 to 10 halves for garnish

½ tablespoon unsalted butter

Equipment: 10-inch springform pan

Preheat oven to 375°F. In a large mixing bowl, beat eggs and sugar with an electric mixer until very thick. Add salt, olive oil and orange zest. Mix thoroughly. Combine persimmon and pawpaw pulps and pears in a separate bowl. Add lemon juice and mix well.

Combine flour and baking powder in a small bowl, then mix dry ingredients thoroughly into the egg mixture. Batter will be stiff. Add the fruit and chopped pecans to the mixture and blend well.

Coat the bottom and sides of the springform pan with butter and pour the batter into it. Shake the pan from side to side to level the batter, but do not press down on it. Gently press the pecan halves lightly around the top of the cake.

Bake for 45 to 50 minutes or until the cake is golden brown and a toothpick inserted into the center comes out clean. This moist cake keeps well for several days if wrapped with foil and refrigerated.

This is adapted from a bread-pudding recipe I learned in Susana Trilling's *Seasons of My Heart* cooking class in Oaxaca, Mexico. There, we made it with fresh pumpkin cubes and topped it with a rich rum sauce. This pudding needs no extravagant adornment. However, if you want to dress it up a bit, I suggest topping each individual serving with a couple of tablespoons of the exquisitely beautiful orange persimmon pulp, letting it pool over onto the serving dish. It's perfect with coffee or rooibos chai tea.

persimmon bread pudding

Serves 8 to 10

4 cups milk

½ cup butter

2 tablespoons rum

½ cup golden raisins

4 eggs

1½ cups sugar

1 teaspoon ground nutmeg

1 teaspoon cinnamon

2 teaspoons vanilla extract

¼ teaspoon salt

2 cups persimmon pulp (rendered from processing about 3 pounds whole persimmons)

6 cups stale, firm-textured bread cubes with crusts

⅔ cup chopped pecans

Preheat oven to 350°F. Scald milk in medium saucepan. Melt butter in milk and let mixture cool for 10 minutes.

In a small saucepan, heat the rum, 2 tablespoons water and raisins. Simmer over low heat for 10 minutes or until liquid has evaporated.

In a large bowl, mix the eggs, sugar, nutmeg, cinnamon, vanilla and salt. Then add milk mixture, whisking constantly while adding so as not to cook the eggs. Add 1 cup persimmon pulp to mixture, reserving remainder for later use. Mix well for 4 or 5 minutes. Add raisins and bread and stir to coat thoroughly.

Pour into a buttered 9- by 12-inch casserole dish and bake for 1¼ hours (covering with foil if the top of the pudding browns too far before it is done). Remove foil, if used, and sprinkle top with pecans during the last 10 minutes of baking; nuts should get lightly toasted.

leave on the crusts

It is not necessary to remove bread crusts. Leaving them attached results in a slightly chewy top crust, which contrasts nicely with the smooth pudding-like texture beneath.

Here's a quick, pretty and light little dessert that you can throw together in 10 or 15 minutes. Pressing the persimmons through the food mill takes only a few minutes, also.

persimmon parfait

Serves 2

1 pound persimmons (about 24)
¼ cup plain or vanilla yogurt (or freshly whipped cream)
1 tablespoon chopped, toasted pecans or hickory nuts
4 gingersnaps, crumbled (optional)

Remove the thin, green-to-brown caps from the persimmons and gently rinse any dirt from the fruit. Force the fruit's pulp through a food mill into a bowl, leaving seeds and skin pieces in the mill. This should yield about ⅔ cup pulp.

In a small, stemmed dish place 3 tablespoons persimmon pulp. On top of that put 2 tablespoons of yogurt. Top with a 2- or 3-tablespoon dollop of persimmon pulp and sprinkle with 1½ teaspoons chopped nuts. Repeat procedure in second dish.

You also may add gingersnap crumbles to the layered mix for a crunchier texture. Vary the proportions as you like. If you have a few gingersnaps, crumble them finely and sprinkle on top of the yogurt, surrounding the pool of persimmon in the middle.

a deep bow to persimmon orange

The deep-orange color of persimmon pulp is one of the most beautiful colors in all of nature, I think. I love to force the little fruits through the food mill as often as possible, just so I can indulge in this visual delight!

163

Hunter-angler-forager Kevin Lohraff shared some mighty tasty persimmon pie with me one day in the office. I was awed by its wonderful custardy texture. He inherited this recipe from his "adopted" granny, Jewell McConnell—a "pie-maker extraordinaire." Kevin has many happy memories of going through several of her remarkable pies every year during deer hunts on the McConnell farm near Bakersfield in Ozark County. I love the economy of effort that she employed as she probably went about doing other household tasks while she let whole persimmons "steep" in the buttermilk.

Jewell McConnell's persimmon pie

Makes 1 pie

Pastry for one 9-inch pie shell

2 cups whole persimmons
2 cups buttermilk
¼ cup sugar
1 egg

2 tablespoons flour
1 teaspoon baking powder
½ teaspoon baking soda
¼ teaspoon cloves
½ teaspoon allspice
1 teaspoon cinnamon
1 tablespoon butter

Preheat oven to 425°F. Roll out the pastry and use it to line a 9-inch pie pan. Set aside.

Remove the thin, greenish-brown caps from the persimmons and gently rinse any dirt from the fruit. Let the fruit and buttermilk stand together in a bowl for 10 minutes; then smash through a colander into another bowl. Set aside. In a separate bowl, beat sugar and egg together until thick. Sift dry ingredients together and blend well into the sugar-egg mixture. Stir the persimmon-buttermilk mixture into all, blending well.

Pour into pie shell and dot top of pie with pieces of the butter. Bake for 10 minutes, then reduce the heat to 300°F and bake until a knife inserted slightly off-center comes out clean.

I love to put this gelato between gingersnap cookies to make little bite-sized sandwiches. Because persimmon pulp tends to be rather dense, I add a bit more liquid to this gelato mixture than I do when using other kinds of fruits. See page 148 for more details about making gelato.

persimmon frozen-yogurt gelato

Serves 6 to 8

1 pound persimmon pulp (about 2 cups pulp rendered from processing about 3 pounds of whole persimmons)

1 cup sugar

1 cup water

1 cup plain yogurt

Whisk pulp and sugar together in a metal bowl until thoroughly blended. Then add water and blend well again. Whisk yogurt gently into the fruit mixture, combining thoroughly. Taste; the fresh-fruit flavor should shine through. Add more sugar if you find the mixture isn't sweet enough. Cover bowl and chill for at least 1 hour. I often leave it overnight in the refrigerator.

Pour into the container of your ice-cream maker and freeze, following the manufacturer's instructions. Garnish with gingersnap cookies.

These started out to be muffins, but at the last minute I decided to pour the batter into a previously unused mini Bundt-cake pan that had been taking up real estate in my kitchen pantry for 20 years. I loved the look of the little ridged rings and decided a light drizzle of glaze would accentuate their curves even more. Make some coffee or tea, light a fire in the fireplace, and invite over your six best friends to savor these as you watch the oak leaves drop outside your window.

persimmon Bundt cakes
with maple-bourbon glaze

Makes 6 mini Bundt cakes or 12 muffins

⅓ cup golden raisins
1 cup unbleached white flour
1 cup whole-wheat flour
2 teaspoons baking powder
¼ teaspoon baking soda
1 teaspoon ground cinnamon
½ teaspoon ground ginger
¼ teaspoon ground allspice
¼ teaspoon ground cloves
½ teaspoon salt
½ cup canola oil
1 cup sugar
1 cup persimmon pulp
¼ cup buttermilk
2 large eggs
1 teaspoon pure vanilla extract
3 tablespoons chopped black walnuts

Equipment: "Mini" Bundt cake tin or muffin tin

Preheat oven to 400°F. Butter Bundt or muffin pans if not nonstick or line muffin pans with individual paper baking cups. Soak raisins in hot water 5 minutes, then drain.

Meanwhile, whisk together flours, baking powder, baking soda, spices and salt in a large bowl.

In a separate bowl, whisk together oil, sugar, persimmon pulp, buttermilk, eggs and vanilla. Add to dry ingredients and stir until just combined, then stir in raisins and walnuts.

Divide batter among Bundt or muffin cups and bake until a wooden toothpick comes out clean, about 15 minutes. Cool on a rack and drizzle with glaze.

maple-bourbon glaze

2 tablespoons unsalted butter
¼ cup pure maple syrup
½ cup powdered sugar
1 teaspoon bourbon
2 teaspoons heavy cream

In a small saucepan, heat butter and syrup together over medium-low heat until butter is melted. Whisk powdered sugar into hot mixture until smooth. Add bourbon and cream, whisking quickly to blend. Immediately pour over cooled cakes.

make your own powdered sugar

If you find that you don't have powdered sugar on hand, don't despair. You very quickly can make your own. For each cup of powdered sugar, add one cup of regular granulated sugar to the blender. Blend until it turns into a powder.

sifting baking soda

At the risk of sounding overly fussy, I always sift baking soda prior to adding it to other ingredients. If you've ever had the unfortunate experience of biting into a cookie or piece of cake that didn't have the dry ingredients sifted together or well blended, you'll know what I mean. Even when I'm using only a tiny amount of soda, I smash it through a small mesh strainer just to make sure there won't be any unpleasant globs to ruin my desserts.

This one's a real buffet show-stopper, and so much fun to make and assemble. When Condé Nast Publishing announced that the November 2009 issue of *Gourmet* would be the last, those of us who had been loyal readers for decades were saddened. As I thumbed through that final issue, the pumpkin-gingerbread trifle recipe called out to me. I decided to honor my constant magazine companion of 35 years by making the dessert for Thanksgiving dinner. It was so delicious and elegant that I adapted the recipe to use a month later with persimmon pulp I had in the freezer. It worked just as beautifully, and was a lovely centerpiece at a Slow Food Katy Trail holiday brunch in December that featured local foods.

persimmon-gingerbread trifle

Serves 12 to 20

Gingerbread

2 cups unbleached white flour

1 teaspoon baking soda

2 teaspoons ground ginger

½ teaspoon ground cinnamon

½ teaspoon salt

1 stick unsalted butter, softened

1 cup packed brown sugar

1 large egg

½ cup sorghum (or mild molasses; *not* blackstrap)

¾ cup buttermilk

½ cup hot water

Persimmon mousse

1¼-ounce envelope unflavored gelatin

¼ cup cold water

2 cups persimmon pulp

½ cup packed brown sugar

½ teaspoon ground cinnamon

½ teaspoon grated nutmeg

½ teaspoon grated fresh ginger root

⅛ teaspoon salt

1 cup chilled heavy cream

½ teaspoon pure vanilla extract

Whipped cream

1½ cups chilled heavy cream

3 tablespoons sugar

1 teaspoon pure vanilla extract

Garnish: chopped crystallized ginger
    and toasted hazelnuts

Equipment: 2-quart trifle bowl or other
        straight-sided, clear-glass bowl

Make gingerbread

Set rack in middle of oven and preheat to 350°F. Butter a 9- by 13-inch baking pan. Line pan with foil, leaving an overhang at both ends; then butter foil.

Whisk together flour, baking soda, spices and salt.

Beat butter and brown sugar with an electric mixer at medium speed until pale and fluffy, 3 to 5 minutes. Beat in egg until blended; then beat in sorghum and buttermilk. At low speed, mix in flour mixture until smooth; then add hot water and beat 1 minute. Wash beaters before making the mousse.

Spread batter evenly in pan and bake 35 to 40 minutes until a toothpick inserted into center comes out clean. Cool in pan. Gently pull up on foil to transfer gingerbread to a cutting board. Cut into 1-inch cubes with a serrated knife.

Make persimmon mousse

Sprinkle gelatin over cold water in a small saucepan and let soften 1 minute. Bring to a simmer, stirring until gelatin has dissolved. Whisk together gelatin mixture, persimmon pulp, brown sugar, spices and salt in a large bowl until combined well.

Beat cream with vanilla until it holds soft peaks, then fold into persimmon mixture gently, but thoroughly.

Make whipped cream

Beat cream with sugar and vanilla until it holds soft peaks.

Assemble trifle

Put half of gingerbread cubes in trifle bowl. Top with half of persimmon mousse, then half of whipped cream. Repeat layering once more with all remaining components. Chill trifle at least 2 hours before serving. Garnish with pieces of crystallized ginger and nuts.

Note: Gingerbread (uncut) can be made 1 day ahead and kept in pan (covered, once cool) at cool room temperature. Trifle, without the top layer of whipped cream, can be made 1 day ahead and chilled; whip half of cream just before serving.

measuring persimmon pulp

3 pounds of whole persimmons make about 2 cups (1 pound) of pulp
Two dozen whole persimmons weigh about 1 pound

grating fresh ginger root

Grated fresh ginger root is essential for the wonderful flavor it lends to this mousse. A microplane grater makes this a less-than-a-minute task, and the difference in taste more than repays your effort. Once you've used one of these graters, you'll never know how you lived without it!

These are two fruits that you are unlikely to find fresh in Missouri at the same time. Gooseberry season usually is ending by the time blueberries begin ripening. However, should you have socked away a few bags in your freezer during the picking season for each, you can make this quick little treat when the cold wind blows. That's what I did on Groundhog Day 2011 after an 18-inch snow fell in Columbia the day before. It was a sweet-tart reminder of warmer temperatures to come.

gooseberry-blueberry crunch

Serves 6 to 8

4 cups gooseberries
2 cups blueberries
1 cup sugar
½ cup flour
1 teaspoon cinnamon
1 teaspoon lemon juice
½ cup water

Topping
½ cup flour
½ cup brown sugar
¼ cup rolled oats
¼ cup butter, melted
½ cup chopped nuts (pecans, walnuts or combination)

Preheat oven to 375°F. In a large bowl, combine gooseberries, blueberries, sugar, flour, cinnamon, lemon juice and water; mix well. Pour into a greased 8½- by 8½-inch baking dish.

In a small bowl, combine flour, brown sugar, oats, butter and nuts. Sprinkle topping over fruit. Bake for about 1 hour or until berries bubble, top is nicely browned, and mixture is set.

fresh or frozen, sweet or tart

The amount of sugar in this recipe makes for a slightly tart result. Should you like things a little sweeter, add a bit more sugar. If nature has allowed for both berries to be available concurrently, then, by all means, try this dessert with the fresh fruit. However, frozen berries work well, and there is no need for thawing, either.

The marriage of foods, as with people, often is the result of a serendipitous meeting. This was the case one mid-June afternoon when a few red stalks of rhubarb from a farmers-market purchase and a little bowl of just-picked gooseberries found themselves together on my kitchen counter. With just a little spice added, it was a heavenly union.

gooseberry-rhubarb chutney

Makes 1 cup of chutney

1 cup gooseberries
¾ cup sugar
4 tablespoons red-wine or sherry vinegar
1½-inch cinnamon stick
2 teaspoons minced fresh ginger root (peeled)
1 teaspoon lemon juice
1 teaspoon chopped lemon rind, pith removed
Pinch ground cardamom
1 teaspoon minced garlic
Healthy pinch of cayenne pepper
⅔ cup coarsely chopped rhubarb
1 tablespoon golden raisins
1 green onion, chopped
1 tablespoon coarsely chopped almonds, toasted

Stir first 10 ingredients (through cayenne pepper) in medium saucepan over medium heat until sugar dissolves and mixture boils. Lower heat and simmer 20 minutes. Add rhubarb, raisins and onion. Bring to a boil, then simmer 4 to 6 minutes. Add nuts and remove from heat.

Keeps for months in the refrigerator.

great with Indian-spiced venison

This chutney is a delicious accompaniment to venison tenderloin that has soaked in an Indian-inspired marinade. I made such a marinade in a few minutes one morning and grilled the venison that evening. Here's how: I cut a small venison tenderloin into five pieces, put it in a glass bowl with a couple of tablespoons of plain yogurt. Then I poured in a couple of tablespoons of olive oil and a healthy squeeze from a big, fresh lemon. I added pinches of salt, pepper, fresh cardamom, cinnamon, cloves and cayenne. I marinated the venison for 8 hours, then threw it on the grill for a few minutes. It was yummy with the chutney and saffron rice.

tasty as a spread, too

Make a quick appetizer by spreading chutney on crackers or bread with fresh goat cheese.

S avored as a dessert in the British Isles for centuries, a fool usually is made by folding puréed fruit into whipped cream. Yogurt lightens the calorie load here in this quick and easy treat. The color of the purée depends upon whether you use ripe (rose-colored) berries or green ones.

gooseberry fool

Serves 2

1 cup gooseberries
⅓ to ½ cup sugar
¼ cup water
½ cup firm vanilla yogurt

Wash berries thoroughly and drain. Combine them with sugar and water, and bring to a slow boil. Simmer until they are cooked through but not yet mushy. Stir occasionally and taste for sweetness. Let cool in the syrup.

Pour mixture through a fine mesh strainer, pressing pulp through with the back of a wooden spoon. Be sure to scrape in any pulp that may be clinging to the outside of the strainer. Chill for an hour and fold gently into the yogurt, leaving visible streaks of berries and yogurt. Pour mixture into small, stemmed dessert dishes and serve.

no stems or tails

I admit that stemming gooseberries is a tedious task and that I've rejected traditional technique by not doing so here. However, I've found that the beauty of pressing gooseberry pulp through a sieve is that it eliminates the need to fuss with removing stems and tails. Try it and see what you think. Needless to say, you can't get away with this when making a pie!

the berry in need of a marketing campaign

Gooseberries are underestimated, I think—maybe for the same reason persimmons sometimes are. They remain untried because of preconceived ideas. People with such notions, obviously, have never met a warm slice of gooseberry pie with ice cream. I formed my appreciation for the beautiful little striped orbs as a child—picking many a berry, at my mother's insistence, from a neighbor's shrubs. She always rewarded my morning among the thorns, however, with a delicious cobbler in the evening. When I bought my house, I was delighted to find a nice gooseberry patch growing in my backyard.

Here's a sweet treat I invented one day when I had a pint of gooseberries that needed to be used. Punishing temperatures in the high 90s made the thought of turning on the oven to make a pie out of the question. With Italian gelato shops and carts as my inspiration (those Italians make gelato out of every conceivable fruit and nut; see page 148), I came up with this frozen dessert. Not only did I not have to use the oven, but neither did I have to pick stems and tails off the berries. I just tossed them into the saucepan and let the strainer capture the undesirable pieces.

gooseberry frozen-yogurt gelato
with rhubarb sauce

Serves 4

2 cups gooseberries
1 cup sugar
½ cup water
1 cup plain lowfat yogurt

Bring berries, sugar and water to a slow boil. Simmer until berries are soft and juices are slightly thickened, 20 to 30 minutes. Using a wooden spoon, press mixture through a fine-mesh strainer into a small metal bowl. Make sure you scrape the pulp from the outside of the strainer into the bowl. The mixture will yield about a cup of rose-colored syrup. Cool by setting bowl into a slightly larger metal bowl filled with ice.

Once mixture has cooled, stir in yogurt until well blended. Taste; the fresh-fruit flavor should shine through. Add more sugar if you find the mixture isn't sweet enough. Cover bowl and chill for at least 1 hour. I often leave it overnight in the refrigerator.

Freeze according to the manufacturer's instructions for your ice-cream maker. Spoon into dishes and top with *Rhubarb Sauce* (optional).

wait, wait ... don't tell me

Surprise your friends with this gelato; make them guess the kind of fruit it is. Its pale, creamy color belies the berries' original green-to-rose hues. The color of this gelato, of course, depends upon the ripeness of the berries. Gooseberries with a rose-colored blush will yield a pinkish dessert, while green berries will yield a creamy white color.

rhubarb sauce

3 cups rhubarb (about a dozen 10-inch-long slender stalks), cut into ¾-inch chunks
1 cup sugar
1 tablespoon lemon juice

Put all in a small saucepan and bring to a slow boil. Simmer until fruit is soft and mixture becomes a thickened sauce—approximately 15 minutes. Cool.

Mushrooms

mushrooms
fungi beckon the spirits of the gatherer and the cook

Missourians have an insatiable appetite for mushrooms. They love to forage for them, identify them and, quite often, cook with them. The demand for a 12-page mushroom-identification publication produced by the Conservation Department in 1983 has been nearly relentless; so have the sales of the agency's new book, *Missouri's Wild Mushrooms* by Maxine Stone.

Maxine, a 20-year member and past-president of the Missouri Mycological Society (MOMS), probably speaks for many mushroom enthusiasts when she explains her passion for the state's fungi:

"I have always been a gatherer—picking up shells on the beach, rocks, mushrooms—anything. Mushrooming is wonderful for those who have a gatherer's spirit and it's perfect for anyone who is a gatherer *and* who loves good food. You gather mushrooms, come home, and cook and eat them.

"I love to be in the woods looking and exploring," says Maxine. "I like mushroom hunting more than just about anything—searching for both edible and non-edible species. Of course, my heart does extra flutters when I run across a nice patch of chanterelles or other edibles."

Maxine lists several dozen edible native mushrooms in her book and includes 24 recipes, as well. *Missouri's Wild Mushrooms* is available at Conservation nature centers and other booksellers statewide. You also may order at *www.mdcnatureshop.com* or by calling toll free: 1-877-521-8632.

be sure before you eat

Before you eat any wild mushroom, have an expert confirm its identification. Instead of the edible mushroom you think you have, you may have an uncommon poisonous look-alike. Finding a mushroom expert may not be easy, but the Missouri Mycological Society is a good place to start.

Mycologists Walter Sundberg and Andrew Methven ponder over the identification of an obscure mushroom. It, along with hundreds of other fungi, were collected and identified during the MOMS annual weekend foray at Mingo Wildlife Refuge. Many turned up a few hours later in delicious dishes at the after-the-hunt feast.

calling all mushroom enthusiasts

Perhaps you've tasted your first morel and that experience has motivated you to forage for your own fungi. Maybe you've taken an autumn walk in the woods, been amazed at the abundance of fungi, and want to know more about what you've seen. For years, possibly, you've been wondering if the "toadstools" in your yard are deadly or delicious. Becoming a member of the Missouri Mycological Society (MOMS) is a great way to quench your thirst for mushroom knowledge.

Founded in 1987, this organization's goal is to foster and expand the understanding of mushrooms through studying and enjoying them. It is one of about 100 such amateur mushroom clubs affiliated with the North American Mycological Association.

MOMS sponsors frequent forays, identification classes and other educational activities. The annual events calendar posted on its excellent website shows what an active and interesting group MOMS is. I also can testify to the many creative cooks among the members. Their after-the-hunt dinners and winter luncheons—laden with fabulous mushroom dishes—are among the many reasons to mingle with these mushroomers.

The society leans toward the St. Louis area, but includes members from throughout Missouri and southwestern Illinois. Chapters recently have been established in the Columbia-Jefferson City area and in Springfield.

The MOMS Education and Research Committee continues to do research on the growing habits of morels and chanterelles. Specimens are stored at the Dunn-Palmer Herbarium at the University of Missouri-Columbia. In addition, all mushrooms that have been found in Missouri are listed on the MOMS website.

More details about the Missouri Mycological Society abound at: www.MoMyco.org.

An overabundance of needing-to-be-used vegetables in my fridge one summer evening inspired me to come up with this combination. I also had picked chanterelles earlier in the day, so I wanted to make use of those, as well. The hickory nuts were the perfect crunchy complement to the earthy, smoky vegetables. You may vary the kinds and amounts of vegetables to suit your taste.

spaghetti with grilled summer vegetables, chanterelles and hickory nuts

Serves 4

⅓ cup hickory nuts

2 cups fresh chanterelles

3 small zucchini, green and/or yellow

2 medium fresh sweet peppers, red and/or green

8 small okra

1 medium eggplant

1 medium onion

5 tablespoons extra-virgin olive oil

15 cherry tomatoes, any size or color combination

¾ pound whole-wheat spaghetti

2 garlic cloves, minced

4 tablespoons finely chopped fresh parsley, chives and basil

¾ cup grated Romano or Parmigiano-Reggiano cheese

Salt and coarsely grated pepper to taste

Toast hickory nuts lightly in a skillet or toaster-oven. Set aside. Clean mushrooms of debris, dry, chop into large pieces and set aside.

Cut squash and peppers into 1½-inch pieces, and okra, eggplant and onion into 1-inch pieces. Toss vegetables in a bowl with 4 tablespoons olive oil, then thread them on metal or bamboo skewers (bamboo skewers must be soaked in water 30 minutes before placing on grill). It's a good idea to thread each skewer with the same vegetable (eggplant on one, peppers on another, for instance), so an entire skewer can be removed if one of the vegetables is cooking more quickly than others.

Heat grill to medium-high and put on a pot of water to boil for pasta. When grill is hot, put on vegetable skewers (except for tomatoes). Turn skewers every few minutes to cook vegetables evenly.

When vegetables are halfway cooked, add pasta to boiling water. As it cooks, add 1 tablespoon olive oil to a small pan and sauté garlic and mushrooms. Stir frequently and cook for just a few minutes, until mushrooms are tender. Turn off the heat and let mushrooms rest while vegetables finish cooking on the grill. Add tomato skewers to the grill during the last minute or two of grilling time; turn gently and cook just until heated through. Remove all vegetables from skewers to a bowl. Cover to keep warm.

Toss herbs, cheese, nuts and mushrooms in serving bowl. Add all vegetables and toss again. Drain pasta, reserving 1 tablespoon of water. Add pasta, reserved water, salt and pepper to the bowl of vegetables and toss again. Taste for seasoning and serve.

plane graters are the best

Nothing beats a stainless-steel plane grater for
shredding hard cheeses, such as Romano and
Parmigiano-Reggiano, into fluffy little piles. I hold
mine with one hand while tilting it at a comfortable
angle to make contact with the cutting board. A little
rubber foot keeps it from sliding as I grate cheese.
Plane graters are very sharp, so exercise caution!

I had just taken a trout out of the smoker one July evening when my friend, Dory Colbert, dropped by with a bag of chanterelles from her yard. I made bruschette with the trout and chanterelles that evening, and used the same duo in this pasta the next night. Experiment with the amount of half and half in this dish. You may want more if you like your pasta saucy. I prefer pasta (especially handmade or good-quality dried) and the main ingredients in the dish to be up front. Consequently, I use a little less sauce so the flavors aren't obscured.

fettuccine with chanterelles and smoked trout

Serves 2 as a main dish or 4 as a first course

2 tablespoons extra-virgin olive oil

2 tablespoons butter

⅓ cup chopped onion

2 sprigs of thyme, chopped

1 teaspoon chopped chives

2 tablespoons chopped parsley

8 ounces chanterelles

Salt and freshly ground pepper

4 ounces smoked trout, broken into bite-sized pieces

¾ to 1 cup half and half

1 tablespoon fresh lemon juice

A few gratings of fresh nutmeg

8 ounces fettuccine

Heat olive oil and butter in large sauté pan. Sauté onion and herbs until onion softens, 2 to 3 minutes. Add chanterelles, a pinch of salt and pepper, and cook 5 minutes or until the mushrooms release their juices.

Stir in trout, half and half, and heat 1 or 2 minutes until thickened. Add lemon juice and nutmeg and mix thoroughly. Toss with freshly cooked and drained pasta. Serve immediately.

saving chanterelles for later

Have you ever stumbled upon a mother lode of chanterelles and can't use them all? Lucky you! If you just can't eat any more and all your friends have been gifted, why not preserve some for later use? Sauté the mushrooms in butter with a little onion and freeze them in resealable bags.

Outdoor food markets have been a lifelong attraction for me, and in just about every place I travel or visit, I'll make my way to one. While roaming one morning amidst the teeming tables of gorgeous goods at a Portland, Oregon farmers market, I came across a table piled high with local mushrooms. Behind a mountain of lovely chanterelles was chef Kathryn LaSusa Yeomans of Sage Culinary Advice, who was offering samples of these mouth-watering bruschette. She kindly parted with her recipe, and I encourage you to give it a try with Missouri chanterelles.

chanterelle and smoked-salmon bruschette

Serves 6

3 tablespoons extra-virgin olive oil, plus more for toasting the bread

¾ pound chanterelle mushrooms, cleaned of forest debris and chopped into bite-sized pieces

Salt and freshly ground pepper to taste

2 tablespoons butter

1 large shallot, finely chopped

2 garlic cloves, 1 minced and the other cut in half

1 shot (1 ounce) of brandy

6 ounces hot-smoked salmon (not lox), flaked

¼ cup sour cream (optional)

A loaf of rustic bread, such as ciabatta

Over a high heat, heat the olive oil in a skillet large enough to accommodate all of the mushrooms in a single layer. (If you do not have a pan this large, cook the mushrooms in batches and combine them before adding the butter.) When the oil is very hot—shimmering, but not smoking—add the mushrooms all at once and cook over high heat, stirring occasionally, until any water the mushrooms exude has cooked off and the mushrooms again begin to sizzle.

Reduce the heat to medium and season the mushrooms with salt and pepper. Stir in the butter, then add the shallot and garlic. Continue to cook until the shallot has softened and the mushrooms begin to brown, about 4 minutes. Add the brandy to the mushroom mixture. Cook until the brandy has reduced, adjust seasonings with salt and pepper, and add the smoked salmon and sour cream. Heat until all is warm; do not boil.

Slice bread into 1-inch pieces (or thicker if desired). Brush one side of each slice with olive oil, season with salt, and either grill the bread or place it in a 400°F oven (or under the broiler) until nicely browned. Rub each piece of bread with the halved garlic clove. Top with the mushroom-salmon mixture and serve.

you say tomato, I say chanterelle

This simple and tasty appetizer can be assembled quickly. Chanterelles make a delightful alternative to the more common summer bruschetta topping of fresh tomatoes. In spring, of course, try them with morels.

There's almost nothing I can think of that is so deliciously rewarding for the little time it takes to put together. If you have access to ready-made crusts, then you can have delicious pizza in the time it takes to light the grill, chop and sauté a few ingredients and relax for a few minutes while it cooks. Sometimes I make my own dough, but more often I rely upon a local bakery's delicious whole-wheat pizza crusts when I want to eat quickly. In the summer's heat, I make pizza on my gas grill. It doesn't yield quite the same result as cooking in a wood-fired oven, but it beats heating up the kitchen when it's hot outside! I never make the same pizza twice; instead, I see pizza making as an opportunity to use whatever vegetables, meat and cheese I have on hand. Here's one of my favorites that resulted from a morning's abundant picking of chanterelles.

Missouri chanterelle and prosciutto pizza

Serves 2 as a hearty main dish

2 8-inch whole-wheat pizza crusts

2 tablespoons extra-virgin olive oil, plus extra for drizzling

1 large onion, sliced

2 garlic cloves, minced

3 cups chanterelles, cleaned of forest debris and chopped into bite-sized pieces

2 ounces prosciutto (or bacon), thickly cut and torn or chopped into bite-sized pieces

Salt and freshly ground pepper to taste

1 ounce Parmigiano-Reggiano cheese, grated

Equipment: A pizza stone or a double layer of unglazed quarry tiles

Place pizza stone or a double layer of quarry tiles on cold grill or in cold oven. Heat to 500°F. Meanwhile, heat olive oil in a medium pan or skillet over medium heat. Add onion and garlic and sauté until soft. Add mushrooms and cook briefly until tender, stirring frequently. Add prosciutto, salt and pepper and cook for just a minute or two, stirring frequently.

Place pizza crusts on rimless cookie sheet and drizzle each with olive oil, spreading evenly with fingers to coat crusts lightly. Turn contents of sauté pan onto the 2 crusts, dividing mixture evenly between them. Top each with cheese and again drizzle olive oil lightly over the tops. Slide pizza onto hot tiles on grill or in oven. Close grill cover and bake until bottoms of crusts are lightly charred, about 7 or 8 minutes.

a pizza a week—different and delicious every time

A weekly pizza has become one of my favorite summer rituals—especially when the tomatoes and basil are coming on fast. Fresh heirloom tomatoes snuggled up against fresh mozzarella, and topped with roughly torn fresh basil can't be beat. It's amazing how quickly you can top a disk of dough, throw it on to cook, and be eating in less than 30 minutes from when you entered the kitchen. You can use a wide range of ingredients and it will turn out fabulously. It's a great way to clean out the refrigerator's vegetable bin of slightly sagging zucchini, onion, kale and peppers. Use smoked fish, venison or wild-game sausage, or go vegetarian with morels, chanterelles or other local, edible mushrooms. Sprinkle all with Parmigiano-Reggiano or Romano cheese.

notes from a hot place!

Here's a little advice from one who knows about burned pizza crusts: Because of the high heat required to cook the pizza on top and make a crisp crust on the bottom, you'll need some insulation between the bottom of the crust and the grill or oven rack. Get yourself either a pizza stone or unglazed quarry tiles (in sizes to fit your oven or grill in the configuration of your choice). I use a dozen 6- by 6-inch tiles double stacked to create about a ⅞-inch thickness. The resulting surface area is 18 inches long by 12 inches wide and it works like a charm.

I've had the tiles for 15 years and got them originally to use in my oven to bake bread. They spend the summer on the grill and they winter in the oven; I simply move them out of the way in either place when not needed. Alternatively, you may use a pizza stone, available in most kitchen shops. The idea is to evenly distribute the heat (mimicking the effects of baking in a masonry oven) and not burn the crusts beyond edibility.

Here's a quick and delicious camping dish from mushroom enthusiast David Yates. It also works just as well at home when baked in a 425°F oven.

chanterelle and polenta foil packs

Serves 4

2 cups fresh chanterelles

2 tablespoons butter

Salt and freshly ground pepper

1 tablespoon extra-virgin olive oil

1 polenta log, purchased
   (or see page 46 to make your own polenta)

4 sprigs fresh rosemary

Clean chanterelles and tear into bite-sized pieces, leaving the very small ones whole. Sauté in butter with salt and pepper to taste for 4 to 5 minutes, or until liquid has evaporated.

Cut 4 12- by 12-inch squares of aluminum foil. Spread olive oil lightly on each piece. Place a slice or two of polenta on foil. Top with chanterelles and a rosemary sprig. Fold up foil and bake over hot coals for about 10 minutes, or a bit longer if you prefer the polenta edges crunchy.

a fungus with a fan club

The chanterelle is reputed to be the most popular edible mushroom in the world, and Missouri is home to three different species. Look for them in summer in our oak-hickory forests—especially after periods of extended rain.

Friend and fabulous cook, Michel Gregory, adapted this recipe from one that called for shiitake mushrooms. It's a delicious and interesting way to enjoy morels.

pea shoot-spinach salad
with bacon and morels

Serves 4 to 6

¾ pound fresh morel mushrooms
4-ounce piece of smoky, meaty bacon
3½ tablespoons extra-virgin olive oil
1 teaspoon coarse salt
1½ tablespoons fresh lemon juice
½ tablespoon red-wine vinegar
½ tablespoon coarse-grain mustard
½ teaspoon freshly ground black pepper
4 ounces (4 cups) fresh pea shoots
4 ounces (4 cups) baby spinach leaves
1 handful fresh chives, cut into 1-inch lengths
8 to 12 pieces of shaved Parmigiano-Reggiano cheese

Clean mushrooms by picking out bugs and dirt; wash only if necessary. Cut into bite-sized pieces.

Cut bacon into ¾-inch-thick matchsticks and cook in a heavy skillet over medium-low heat. Stir until crisp, but still chewy, 6 to 8 minutes. Drain on paper towels.

Pour off fat from skillet and add 1½ tablespoons olive oil, mushrooms and ½ teaspoon salt. Cook over medium heat, stirring occasionally, until mushrooms are golden, 7 or 8 minutes; then cool.

In a large salad bowl, whisk together lemon juice, vinegar, mustard, pepper and remaining ½ teaspoon salt and 2 tablespoons olive oil until well blended.

Add pea shoots and spinach to dressing; toss to coat. Add bacon, mushrooms and chives, and toss again. Garnish with cheese shavings.

ingredient tip

Pea shoots, which make wonderful garnishes and snacks, are the choice leaves and tendrils of young pea plants. Although they can be harvested from any type of edible garden pea, many food enthusiasts prefer the taste of those from edible-podded peas. Look for them at your local farmers market in the spring.

This dish is pure bliss for morel enthusiasts. "The best way to eat it," says creator Maxine Stone, "is right from the pan. Grab a piece of good bread, then dip and scoop. It's great participatory food!"

mushroom lover's creamed morels

Serves 6 to 8

2 cups fresh or 1 handful dried morels

2 tablespoons unsalted butter

2 shallots, finely chopped

1 pint cream (or half and half; however, cream makes it absolutely superb!)

Salt and freshly ground black pepper

2 to 3 tablespoons Marsala (See *Ingredient Tip.*)

Good rustic bread

If using fresh morels, cut each one in half lengthwise. Pick out bugs and dirt, and wash only if necessary. If you have large morels, cut them into smaller pieces—but not too small.

If using dried morels, reconstitute in water. When sufficiently plump, drain mushrooms through a fine strainer and reserve liquid in a small bowl. Squeeze out any liquid from the mushrooms into the strainer over the bowl. Cut mushrooms into pieces as above.

Melt the butter in a large saucepan or skillet. Add shallots and sauté for a few minutes. Add the morels, stir and sauté for a few minutes more. If you have used dried morels, add the morel liquid, being careful not to pour in any sediment that may have slipped through the strainer (it could be sand or bugs).

Cook morels until most of the liquid in the pan has evaporated. Add cream and cook for a few minutes. Add salt and pepper to taste, then Marsala to taste.

Serve in shallow bowls and accompany with bread.

ingredient tip

Marsala, a fortified wine from Sicily, usually is available where wines are sold.

preserving the bounty

Maxine Stone's kitchen shelves are replete with big jars of dried morels and many other kinds of wild Missouri mushrooms. A dehydrator works well for preserving morels, but she also suggests stringing and hanging them in the sun to dry. "Drying intensifies the flavor and odor of the morel. Don't be afraid to experiment," she says.

Here's a light and delicious way that Maxine Stone serves fresh blewit mushrooms.

barley and blewit salad

1 cup pearl barley
2 cups fresh blewit mushrooms, sliced
3 to 4 garlic cloves, chopped
¼ cup, plus 1 tablespoon extra-virgin olive oil
2 tablespoons red-wine vinegar
2 tablespoons tamari
1 teaspoon Dijon mustard
Salt and freshly ground pepper
½ teaspoon freshly ground cumin
4 tablespoons toasted sunflower seeds
¼ cup chopped fresh parsley
¼ cup chopped fresh thyme
4 cups torn Savoy cabbage

Preheat oven to 350°F. Cook barley in water according to directions—usually about an hour. Drain and set aside.

Combine mushrooms, garlic and 1 tablespoon olive oil in a large pan and roast in the oven for about 15 minutes, stirring occasionally. When mushrooms are cooked and garlic is soft, remove from oven and set aside.

Make dressing of ¼ cup olive oil, vinegar, tamari, mustard, salt and pepper; mix well.

In a bowl, combine barley and remaining ingredients. Stir in mushroom mixture. Drizzle with dressing, toss all and serve warm or at room temperature.

blewits in the mulch pile

Check mulch piles in autumn for blewits. If you find a good batch, check the spot again later. A blewit mycelium—the fungi's "roots"—can produce several crops in one season.

There are some fine cooks among the members of the Missouri Mycological Society (MOMS). When they gather for forays throughout the state, they also bring some marvelous mushroom dishes to the after-the-hunt party. Steve Booker, one of the society's directors, created this tasty treatment for hen-of-the-woods mushrooms, which he likes to serve as an appetizer or side dish.

pickled "hens"—Italian style

8 cups hen-of-the-woods mushrooms, cleaned and separated

¼ cup fresh lemon juice

1 onion

2 green peppers

1 red pepper

1 yellow pepper

6 garlic cloves, either chopped or whole

6 anchovy fillets, mashed or crumbled

6 cups water

2 cups vinegar

1½ cups sugar

Place hen pieces in pot and cover with water. Add lemon juice. Bring to a boil and simmer for about 10 minutes. Rinse in cool water, drain and set aside.

Cut onion and peppers into bite-sized pieces, and place in a bowl. Add garlic and anchovies and stir well. Put everything, including mushrooms, into a large pot and add water, vinegar and sugar. Bring to a boil and simmer for about 10 minutes. Remove from heat and cool. Put into clean jars and refrigerate for a week or so before eating.

dining with MOMS

The Incurable Epicureans—a group of MOMS members who love to cook and eat—gather several times a year for dinners with specially planned themes and menus. They dig their forks into various regions of the world, eras or whatever else appeals to their culinary spirits. For more information about joining MOMS, visit their wonderful website at *www.MoMyco.org*.

Passionate mycophile Maxine Stone, who forages throughout Missouri, makes this deliciously rich and "meaty" soup with her freshly gathered hen-of-the-woods mushrooms.

hearty "hen" soup

Serves 4 to 6

2 cups chopped onions

3 tablespoons butter

1 pound hen-of-the-woods mushrooms, cleaned and separated

1 to 2 teaspoons dill

2 cups vegetable stock or water

1 tablespoon tamari

1 to 2 tablespoons Hungarian paprika

3 tablespoons flour

1 cup milk

2 teaspoons fresh lemon juice

Salt and freshly grated pepper

Chopped parsley (optional)

Thick Greek yogurt (optional)

Sauté the onions in 1 tablespoon of butter over medium heat. Add the mushrooms, dill, half the stock or water, tamari and paprika. Cover and simmer for about 15 minutes.

In a large pot, melt the remaining butter. Whisk in flour and cook a few minutes while continuing to whisk. Add milk and cook over low heat until thick, stirring frequently, about 10 minutes. Stir in mushroom mixture, remaining stock, lemon juice, salt and pepper. Cover and let simmer for about 10 more minutes.

Serve hot and garnish, if desired, with chopped parsley and yogurt.

fascinating fungi

Individual clusters of this mushroom—which also is called maitake—can weigh up to 100 pounds, according to Maxine. She says that hens are often found in the same area year after year, so check your spot every autumn. To learn more about Missouri's fascinating fungi, pick up a copy of *Missouri's Wild Mushrooms*, written by Maxine Stone and published by the Missouri Department of Conservation.

sources

Below are publications and websites referred to in the text, as well as others that supplied me with facts or influenced my thinking during this project.

Beard, James. *American Cookery* (Boston: Little, Brown and Company, 1972).

—————. *James Beard's New Fish Cookery* (Boston: Little, Brown and Company, 1976).

Bon Appétit (published monthly).

Bienvenu, Marcelle and Judy Walker, editors. *Cooking Up a Storm: Recipes Lost and Found From The Times-Picayune of New Orleans* (San Francisco: Chronicle Books, 2008).

Borg, Shannon and Lora Lea Misterly. *Chefs on the Farm* (Seattle: Skipstone, 2008).

Brillat-Savarin, Jean-Anthelme. *The Physiology of Taste*. Trans. M.F.K. Fisher (New York: Harcourt Brace Jovanovich, 1949).

Caruso, James Campbell. *El Farol: Tapas and Spanish Cuisine* (Salt Lake City: Gibbs Smith, 2004).

Child, Julia and Simone Beck. *Mastering the Art of French Cooking* (New York: Alfred A. Knopf, 1970).

Claiborne, Craig. *The New York Times Cook Book* (New York: Harper & Row, 1961).

Fisher, M.F.K. *The Art of Eating* (New York: Vintage Books, 1976).

Food & Wine (published monthly).

Frieberg, Carol. *Breakfast in Bed Cookbook* (Seattle: Sasquatch Books, 1990).

Gourmet (formerly published monthly).

Hazan, Marcella. *The Classic Italian Cookbook* (New York: Alfred A. Knopf, 1978).

—————. *More Classic Italian Cooking* (New York: Alfred A. Knopf, 1978).

—————. *Essentials of Classic Italian Cooking* (New York: Alfred A. Knopf, 1992).

Hemmelgarn, Dan and Melinda. *Healing Hands 2011, Celebrating the Farmers Who Nourish Us* (Columbia, Missouri: Enduring Image & Food Sleuth LLC, 2010)

Hildebrand, Caz and Jacob Kenedy. *The Geometry of Pasta* (Philadelphia: Quirk Books, 2010).

Jaffrey, Madhur. *An Invitation to Indian Cooking* (New York: Vintage Books, 1975).

Jamison, Cheryl Alters and Bill Jamison. *The Border Cookbook* (Boston: The Harvard Common Press, 1995).

Kuo, Irene. *The Key to Chinese Cooking* (New York: Alfred A. Knopf, 1977).

Kurz, Don. *Shrubs and Woody Vines of Missouri* (Jefferson City, Missouri: Missouri Department of Conservation, 1997).

—————. *Trees of Missouri* (Jefferson City, Missouri: Missouri Department of Conservation, 2003).

Lewis, Edna. *The Taste of Country Cooking* (New York: Alfred A. Knopf, 1976).

Lind, Mary Beth and Cathleen Hockman-Wert. *Simply in Season* (Scottdale, Pennsylvania: Herald Press, 2005).

Nabhan, Gary Paul, editor. *Renewing America's Food Traditions* (White River Junction, Vermont: Chelsea Green Publishing Company, 2008).

Nagel, Werner O. *Cy Littlebee's Guide to Cooking Fish & Game* (Jefferson City, Missouri: Missouri Department of Conservation, 1991).

Petrini, Carlo, editor. *Slow Food: Collected Thoughts on Taste, Tradition, and the Honest Pleasures of Food* (White River Junction, Vermont: Chelsea Green Publishing Company, 2001).

Phillips, Jan. *Wild Edibles of Missouri* (Jefferson City, Missouri: Missouri Department of Conservation, 1979).

Pollan, Michael. *The Omnivore's Dilemma* (New York: The Penguin Press, 2006).

Saveur (published nine times annually).

Stone, Maxine. *Missouri's Wild Mushrooms* (Jefferson City, Missouri: Missouri Department of Conservation, 2010).

Terry, Bryant. *Vegan Soul Kitchen: Fresh, Healthy, and Creative African-American Cuisine* (Da Capo Press, 2009).

The St. Louis Herb Society. *Herbal Cookery* (Nashville: Favorite Recipes Press, 2009).

Vanderlip, Marcia, food editor. *Columbia Daily Tribune* (published daily).

Waters, Alice. *Chez Panisse Vegetables* (New York: HarperCollins Publishers, 1996).

Elderberry Life • *www.elderberrylife.com*
Epicurious • *www.epicurious.com*
Seasons of My Heart Cooking School • *www.seasonsofmyheart.com*

sources for learning more about eating locally and sustainably

There are countless books, films and websites on these subjects, but here are a few notable ones.

books

Animal, Vegetable, Miracle • Barbara Kingsolver
The Art of Simple Food • Alice Waters
Everything I Want to Do is Illegal: War Stories from the Local Food Front • Joel Salatin
Farmer John's Cookbook, The Real Dirt on Vegetables • Farmer John Peterson and Angelic Organics
Fast Food Nation • Eric Schlosser
Grub: Ideas for an Urban Organic Kitchen • Anna Lappe and Bryant Terry
In Defense of Food: An Eater's Manifesto • Michael Pollan
Manifestos on the Future of Food & Seed • edited by Vandana Shiva
The Omnivore's Dilemma • Michael Pollan
Renewing America's Food Traditions • edited by Gary Paul Nabhan
Simply in Season • Mary Beth Lind and Cathleen Hockman-Wert
Slow Food Nation: Why Our Food Should be Good, Clean and Fair • Carlo Petrini
The Sustainable Kitchen: Passionate Cooking Inspired by Farms, Forests and Oceans • Stu Stein and others

films

Fast Food Nation
Food Inc.
Fresh
The Future of Food
King Corn
The Real Dirt on Farmer John

websites

Center for Food Safety. True Food Network • *www.centerforfoodsafety.org*
Center for a Livable Future (Johns Hopkins School of Public Health): Connects agriculture and public health.
    Links to Pew Commission report on industrial agriculture • *www.jhsph.edu/clf; http://aphg.jhsph.edu*
Consumer Reports: Greener Choices, newsletter and Eco-label definitions • *www.greenerchoices.org*
Food and Water Watch • *www.foodandwaterwatch.org*
Food Sleuth Radio: Helping listeners connect the dots between the food we love, the health we treasure, and
    the agriculture which influences both • *www.kopn.org* (click on Food Sleuth):
Green America (formerly Co-op America): Economic action for a just planet • *www.greenamericatoday.org*
Health Care Without Harm • *www.noharm.org*
Institute for Agriculture and Trade Policy: Links on food and health • *www.iatp.org*
Slow Food Katy Trail • *slowfoodkatytrail.blogspot.com*
Slow Food USA • *www.slowfoodusa.org*
Sustainable Table: See the *Eat Well Guide* to find sustainable local food • *www.sustainabletable.org*

recipe index

Persimmons

mushrooms

Blewits

Chanterelles

Hen-of-the-Woods

Morels

(clockwise) Black-Walnut Chocolate Biscotti,
Date and Nut Bars, Zimmerschied, Papassinos *and*
Craig's Picante Pecans *(see pages 128–131, 141)*

side dishes and accompaniments